WHO'S JU?

By Dania Ramos

Northampton House Press

Cover design by Shawn Yaney. Interior by NHP.
Northampton House Press edition, 2015, ISBN 978-1-937997-61-8.
Library of Congress Control Number: 2014951530.

9 8 7 6 5 4 3 2

Teaching resources, author bio and information about *The Seventh-Grade Sleuths* series are available at: www.daniaramos.com.

For Michael

WHO'S JU?

CHAPTER ONE:
DNA MALFUNCTION

It's not hard evidence. Just a family photo stuck on our silver fridge with a teapot magnet. Case closed.

"Did you hear me, Justina?" Mami says, pronouncing my name with the J making an H sound, the Spanish way. The right way. *Hoosteenah.*

I turn from the picture. "Huh?"

She's stirring sizzling onions in a pan. "I asked for the *sofrito.*"

I open the refrigerator door and scan the top shelf for the container of blended spices. Instead, I find my sister's *Just Like You* doll bundled up in a tiny ski jacket and squished between the milk and orange juice. I grab

1

the miniature version of Delilah from its frigid hiding spot. "What the heck?"

Lah stands in the doorway on tiptoes, hands on her hips. "Ju! Ju! Ju!"

"You sound like an owl," I say.

She marches across the beige ceramic tile and gawks at me with big brown eyes. "Why'd you take Delilah Juniorette out of her igloo?"

I dangle the doll high above her head. "The fridge is for food, not toys."

Lah jumps to snatch her tiny clone out of my hand and smoothes its perfect chestnut waves. Hair that was customized to match hers. She always talks to the doll as if it's alive. "Don't pay attention to Ju. She thinks she's so smart now that she's in seventh grade." She sticks out her tongue then skips into the dining room and crawls underneath the table. No way I was that annoying when I was seven.

"Check for the *sofrito* one shelf down, under the milk," my mother says.

I finally find the jar of homemade seasoning and set it next to her on the smooth stone countertop.

"Thank you, *m'ija*." She straightens the neck strap of the patchwork apron she made for me last year. Mami and my aunt, Titi Nessa, have an online business called The Craft-e-Shop. They sell homemade clothes, accessories made from recycled materials, and hand-painted shoes. I always get tons of cute freebies.

My mother adjusts the flame on the stove. "Now I need the peanut sauce."

"You sure this'll taste good?" I pass her a bottle of yellowish paste.

She gives me a narrow sideways look. "Are you doubting my Thai food experiment?"

"Me? Never."

"Uh-huh." She points at my hand tugging the little silver frog charm hanging on a chain around my neck. "I know you're full of doubt when you're yanking on that *coquí* necklace."

It's true. I fiddle with my frog charm whenever I'm uncertain about something. Nervous habit. I slide my hands into the pockets of my apron and smile. "It'll probably be delicious."

The photo on the fridge catches my eye again. My family at the beach. Mami, Papi, and Lah are tan and smiling. But I'm scowling, amber eyes squinting as if I'm mad about not inheriting my parents' brown hair, brown eyes, and olive skin like my sister did. The picture reminds me of what happened a few days ago in Health Studies. Mrs. Mollick stood in front of the class and said, "Your first major assignment of the year is the Blueprint of Life Project. In order to complete it, you must each solve your own personal mystery." Mrs. Mollick leaned toward us, whispering like she was sharing a big secret. "And the evidence is in your genes."

Ig Soto, my best friend since daycare, had said under his breath, "Easy A."

I'd been thinking the same thing. After all, we're both members of a secret mystery club. At the time, the idea of mapping and sequencing DNA, the microscopic stuff that carries all genetic information, had seemed fine. But now, as I think about studying my *own* DNA, I realize that if this family photo on our fridge is Exhibit A then there's no denying one cold hard fact.

There's a glitch in my blueprint.

I stare at my mother's ponytail of dark brown curls and then tuck my frizzy blond hair behind my ears. "How old do I need to be to dye my hair?"

She laughs. "You want to color it purple?"

"No. Brown."

Mami exhales. She lays the wooden spoon on the stove and clasps my hand. "Justina. You don't need brown hair to be part of this family. Puerto Ricans come in all shades."

"I know. I know." But seeing our fingers intertwined—hers the color of caramel and mine pale as ivory—makes me wonder what it'd be like to match the rest of my family for a change.

It's after dinner and I'm in the living room with my father who's sound asleep on the burgundy sofa. His snore sounds like a tiny train is riding in a circle through his nose and throat. Not the best background noise for a mystery movie about a bloodthirsty dog prowling the moors of England. Maybe it sounds weird, but watching black-and-white mysteries is an old tradition for Papi and me. Except lately, he's been falling asleep halfway through the films. I hit the stop button on the remote and reach for the dimmer knob, twisting it until there's a faint glow in the room. His head is tilted back on the armrest, mouth open.

I brush past the droopy-leafed plant Mami bought him when he made partner at his law firm three months ago. "Pa, you're missing the best part." I give his shoulder a nudge.

He lifts his head. His hair's matted on one side. "Did it finish?"

I shake my head. "Holmes just took off his disguise."

"That's the best part," he says.

"You snored through it."

"Sorry. Got up so early." He grunts as he stands, then drags his feet to the doorway. "I'm going to bed. You should too, *mi rubia.*"

My blond one.

He's called me that for as long as I can remember. But I don't want to be the blond one anymore. "How old do I need to be to dye my hair?"

"Ask your mother." He kisses the top of my head and his mustache scratches my forehead. His heavy footsteps thump up the stairs.

He didn't say I *couldn't* do it. Neither did Mami.

I tiptoe into the powder room and tear open a box of the hair color my mother uses to cover her gray. The label reads Deep Brown.

I tug at a lock of yellow frizz. Yeah, my DNA blueprint malfunctioned.

Now it's time to get rid of the evidence.

CHAPTER TWO:
SEVENTH-GRADE SLEUTHS

After school on Monday, Ig and I stroll by the computer lab in the school library, past rows of towering shelves to our secret meeting spot—an alcove near the biography section. We lounge on the navy blue carpet and wait for the only other member of the mystery club, Gunther Corrie.

Gunther was new last year. He'd only been at our school a few weeks when we found him in this very spot surrounded by a pile of *39 Clues* books. It was his idea for the three of us to form a club and meet in the library every Monday. Last year, he was always the first one to show up. But not today.

I adjust the purple knit hat that's covering last night's hair-dye experiment. I'm not ready to unveil my new look, especially since I couldn't scrub off a few brown blotches of dye from my forehead. There's a shuffling between the stacks. Gunther saunters over wearing a green book bag backwards, so it rests on his stomach. I can't help but smile at his spiky red hair. I hope it isn't totally obvious I think his freckled face is adorable. Especially since Sara Baker is standing next to him, applying a grease slick of lip balm that smells like she's been swimming in a sea of fruit punch.

"Sorry I'm late," Gunther says. "But someone was following me."

Ig stares at Sara, then clutches his dark wavy hair as if he's about to yank it out. "What's she doing here?"

"Hi Ig. Tina." Sara smiles, fluorescent light glaring off her bright-pink lips.

"Not my name," I say.

"But Tina is much less confusing." She eyes me up and down, from purple knit hat to embroidered messenger bag to the painted butterflies on my Mary Jane shoes. "Though I guess if you're going to dress like a weirdo, you need a weirdo name to match."

Gunther slumps onto a footstool a few feet away. "She's got a point about the shoes, Feliciano."

I cross my arms. "They're one-of-a-kind. Hand-painted." I don't mention my aunt's the one who did the painting.

"Why are you here?" Ig asks again.

"I need a favor." Sara blots her lips with a tissue. "From your club."

I glare at her. "What're you talking about?"

"She knew about the club," Gunther says, shrugging. "Don't know how. But she did."

Sara sighs. "This one time last year? I was browsing through the biographies of famous Broadway actors and overheard you guys talking."

Gunther leans his head against the light-gray wall. "And she's got a real mystery."

"You have to help me," she says, looking from Ig to Gunther to me.

Ig shakes his head. "No way."

I mostly agree, but a small part of me is still curious.

Sara peers along the biography aisle then plunks down on the floor next to me. "I'm auditioning for the lead in the school play."

"Yeah, you mentioned it in class. Like, a few hundred times." I yawn.

Sara tosses aside her fuchsia shoulder bag and leans forward. "Well, after auditions were over last Friday and everyone else had already left, I went backstage again. I'd left my sheet music on the piano. That's when I found something really...disturbing. Someone, sort of...wrote my name all over last year's scenery."

"That's the huge mystery?" Gunther smacks a palm on his forehead. "Graffiti? It could've been there for months."

"No." She sighs. "There's evidence that it happened recently."

"What's the big deal?" I dig into my messenger bag, grabbing a pen and a blank notebook. "Get a marker and cross it out."

Sara shakes her head. "Thing is, it isn't exactly written. It's so weird. I can't even explain. If you come backstage, I'll show you."

Ig rolls his eyes. "Sorry. Too busy. We can't."

Sara purses her lips. "If you love mysteries so much you should want to solve mine."

"Look, you're interrupting our meeting," I say.

"What exactly do you do at these things? Chat about the mystery that is your wardrobe?" Sara reaches into her handbag, fishes out a compact mirror, and examines her face.

It's a cold hard fact that we've never once solved an actual mystery. So far.

"How about it?" Gunther shrugs. "Should we help?"

"What good is a mystery club if you don't solve mysteries?" Sara asks.

She's got a point.

Ig is silent. Gunther's nodding but not answering, so I figure I'll speak for the group. "Okay," I say. "We'll check it out."

"*What?*" Ig's mouth hangs open.

Gunther's eyebrows pop up. His face brightens. "We will?"

"But not today. We've got to do some investigative prep work." Not to mention I have to make sure I can get Ig on board. Clearly he's not too thrilled with the idea. At least Gunther seems to be into it.

"Fab." Sara stands and hooks her purse over one shoulder. "Callbacks are about to start, anyway. We can sneak backstage one day during lunch."

"When do you think they'll be done renovating in the cafeteria?" Gunther asks.

"Cafeto*rium*." Sara corrects. "The old cafeteria didn't have a huge stage on one end."

"Whatever it's called. Who cares?" Gunther huffs. "They need to finish soon. It's weird eating with those tarps hanging over all the windows. And they really gotta do something about the gross mouse problem."

Sara lets out a little shriek. "What mouse problem?"

"Bernstein and O'Doul saw a gigantic gray one run behind the drink machines." He shudders. "Ugh. Doesn't it creep you out just imagining it crawling all over the—"

"Stop!" Sara slaps at her legs as if a ghost mouse is crawling up.

Ig snorts. "There aren't any in the library, you know. No food allowed." He nods and rubs his chin. "Except food for thought."

"Haha. Funny." Sara clears her throat. "Tomorrow won't work for me. Let's plan on going backstage this Wednesday. Catch you then." And she twirls off down the biography aisle, as if she's exiting stage left.

I turn to my fellow detectives. "How about that? We're finally on a real case."

Gunther nods. "Yeah."

But Ig just sits there with his arms crossed. "Two votes to one. Guess I lose."

"Come on, Ig," I say. "It'll be fun."

"Yeah, Soto." Gunther nudges Ig's leg with his foot. Then in a melodramatic voice he says, "To catch...a vandal. Dum-dum-dum!"

All three of us laugh.

"If we're doing this for real though," Gunther says, "don't we need a name?"

I jot down the first thing that pops into my head. "How about this?" Both stare at what's scrawled across the cover of my notebook.

Official Casebook
of the 7th Grade Sleuths

"Cool." Gunther is grinning so hard the freckles on his cheeks smush together.

Ig's trying hard not to smile, but I know he's excited about the idea, even though our first case is for bigheaded Sara Baker. "Yeah, that works."

On the first page of the notebook I write:

THE CASE OF THE BACKSTAGE VANDAL

Incident: Drama club scenery was vandalized with victim's name

Victim: Sara Baker

Investigators: Gunther Corrie, Ju Feliciano, Ig Soto

Clues:

Clues? Well, we'll get to that on Wednesday.

CHAPTER THREE:
AFTER SCHOOL

fter our meeting in the library, I go over Ig's place to play dominoes. He lives on the first floor of a multi-family house with his mother, sister, and brother. Even though their apartment is way smaller than our house, it's one of the most comfortable places to hang out. Especially the super-bright orange kitchen, where we're seated at a table right now, hovering over our seven tiles. I place the double-six domino in the center and take a sip of hot coffee Ig made. It's light and sweet, like always. Today I ended up with the Jupiter coffee mug. Ig's is Neptune. He's got an entire set, all eight planets. He's really into outer space.

Ig studies his tiles. "I can't believe we're helping Sara Baker. Ms. Diva-of-the-Century. It's like you forgot she's your enemy."

"Yeah, she gets on our nerves, but it's a real mystery to solve," I say. "It makes sense that she asked for our help."

Ig grunts and plays the six blank.

Christina, Ig's sister, stomps into the kitchen typing on her phone. "Did Ma say when she's getting home from class?"

Ms. Soto works full-time and then attends nursing school at night.

He shrugs. "Late."

Christina doesn't take her eyes off the little screen. "But Javier's coming home soon, right?"

"Can you stop texting for one freaking second?" Ig digs his nails into his arm, leaving a row of small moon-shaped indents in his bronze-colored skin.

She glares and tugs at the hem of her denim mini-skirt. "What's your, like, problem?"

"Ma says it's rude to use the phone when you're having a conversation."

"Oh, please. You aren't Ma." She scrunches her thick curly black hair and forces a smile. "Hi, Ju."

"Hey." I take my next turn hoping they don't drag me into the argument.

"I'm going to eat pizza with friends." Christina yanks open the fridge. "There's leftovers you can heat up. Chicken and rice. Enough for you guys and Javi."

15

"Oh, I'm not staying for dinner," I say.

"Whatever." She goes back to texting and clomps out of the room.

Ig slides a domino onto the end closest to him. "I wish you and Gunther would come to your senses and forget about Sara's case. Just like I wish I could forget about..." He shakes his head. "Never mind."

What's up with him? He's not usually this moody. "Something wrong?"

"I'm thinking about getting out of the stupid genetics assignment."

That doesn't sound like Ig. He's pretty much the perfect student. "Why would you do that?"

He bites his lip. "You wouldn't understand."

"Um, hello? Best friend since daycare here. I always understand."

"This is different." He smacks two dominoes together making the ceramic tiles click like two balls on a pool table. "You know both your parents."

"Oh." I hadn't thought about how hard the genetics project might be for him. Mrs. Mollick eagerly explained how, even though forensic technology now exists to detect genetic make-up, we'd be gathering our evidence the old-fashioned way—by interviewing family members and using primary documents. But Ig's not in contact with his father at all. Ms. Soto is raising him, Christina, and Javier on her own. I can't imagine Mrs. Mollick punishing him for a family situation, though. She's a strict teacher, but not mean.

16

Ig stares into his coffee mug, looking miserable. "I don't want to talk about it."

"Okay." So both the genetics project and the backstage mystery are off the table. What's a safe topic? Of course! My brown hair experiment. I yank my knit hat from my head. "Check it out. Ignore the spots on my forehead where I missed. It's hard to aim with that little applicator."

He gapes at me. "Whoa. Your hair is so...so..."

"Deep brown," I say. "It's the color my mother uses to dye her gray."

"But you don't have—" He lets out something between a snort and a cough, which becomes an all-out laugh. "Gray hair. What made you do it?"

I squish the hat into a ball. "To fit in better with my family."

His laughter fades into a frown of confusion. "What makes you think you don't fit in?"

So much for changing the subject. "Guess all this talk of DNA and genetics made me realize how different I am from them."

Ig looks down and scowls at his dominoes. "Stupid project."

"Yeah." I don't know what else to say. I rub my *coquí* charm with my thumb and pointer finger. Too bad the little frog can't grant wishes. I'd ask for this whole assignment to just disappear.

***

The entire next school day goes by without me getting a chance to talk to Ig about the Blueprint of Life Project. It's not until we're walking home that I can finally bring it up. "Did you talk to Mrs. Mollick?"

He sighs. "Yeah, but it didn't go like I'd hoped."

"That stinks." I adjust my purple hat, wishing I could take it off since the afternoon sun is beaming down on us. But I can't risk anyone besides Ig seeing the blotches of hair dye on my forehead. "You're still doing it then?"

He cracks a stick in two, keeping half and tossing the other. "She says she'll give me full credit for researching my mother's side."

I smile. "That's great."

"Except that the assignment's going to be in the Fall Festival," he says.

"Oh." I see his point. That makes things more complicated. The festival takes place in the gym where all students, teachers, and parents can see the projects on display. It's Ig's favorite event of the school year. But knowing how he feels about this one, he won't want to put it out there for the whole school to see.

"I lose either way." He wipes sweat from his forehead. The Fall Festival might only be a few weeks away, but summer's baking heat is still here.

"Sorry, Ig."

Footsteps rush to catch up to us. Sara bursts in between me and Ig. Springing into a twirling leap, she lands facing us.

"What the heck?" Ig scowls. "You!"

18

"Cast list was just posted." She squeals and claps. "I got the female lead!"

"How lovely." I pull down the hem of my baby tee, which Sara twisted up during her grand entrance. "But next time can you try not scaring us half to death when you share good news?"

She gawks at the design on my shirt. "Is that a *bug?*"

"Lizard," I say. "It's a silkscreen print. One of my aunt's original sketches from her reptile series."

She widens her eyes like I've just told her my shirt was radioactive. "O-kay."

"So." Ig taps one Converse sneaker on the sidewalk. "Was there a point to you practically running us over?"

Sara closes her eyes and presses both hands to her chest. "Now that I'm officially starring in the play, I'm counting on you guys to find the creep responsible for using my name to ruin the scenery. Tomorrow at lunch the investigation begins." She hops backward. "Oh! And did you hear the mouse thing was blown way out of proportion? Word got back to some parents who totally freaked, naturally. The school just sent out an email alert about how it's been taken care of. So maybe you should tell Gunther to stop exaggerating already. Toodle-oo!" She prances into the local deli.

"Toodle-oo!" Ig mimics in a high, squeaky voice. We both laugh for a few moments, until he says, "Hey, my mom told me the environmental center is celebrating the opening of the observatory this weekend. Free

19

public night-sky viewings from their new, huge telescope. Wanna come?"

"Sounds cool. I'll ask my parents." About once a month, Ms. Soto or Christina or Javier take Ig to this environmental center where they have events and activities about the stars or the Milky Way or black holes. I've gone a couple times. Pretty interesting. Of course, I still like watching detective movies better.

He grabs my arm. "Don't you have to get home?"

"Oh, right. It's Tuesday." I almost forgot my sisterly duty. Mami expects me home by 3:30 p.m. to watch Lah. "Thanks for reminding me. I would've so been in trouble. Call you tonight." I turn and break into a sprint to make it home in time to babysit.

THROWBACK: SUMMER BEFORE SEVENTH GRADE WHEN I BECAME A BABYSITTER

That day, my father brought home an extra large pizza, half extra cheese and half pepperoni. At dinner he told us how he'd finally made partner at his law firm. How years of hard work had gotten him to such an important position.

"I'll be getting home later now, niñas," Papi said. "Might have to work some Saturdays, too." He popped a slice of pepperoni into his mouth.

Mami smiled at me. "And so, Justina, you'll watch Delilah on Tuesdays and Thursdays when I work in the basement studio."

I nearly choked on a chunk of mozzarella. "I will?"

She nodded. "You're old enough for this responsibility now."

I peeked over at Lah, who was busy stirring her Sprite with a fork. That's when it hit me. Things would be changing for everyone in my family.

Everyone, except my spoiled little sister.

CHAPTER FOUR:
TEA TIME

At home, Lah is waiting for me in her room with everything set up on a little white table. "You're wearing a hat," she says, with a frown that takes up half of her face.

"Yeah, and you're wearing, um..." I squint, trying to make sense of my sister's outfit.

Two pencils are stuck into her ponytail. Her Piglet robe is inside-out, the silky red lining showing. "My Japanese tea outfit!" My sister believes she knows all about Japanese and English tea traditions simply because her friend Chloe has a dad from Japan and a British mom.

Lah has two tea sets. Well, sort of. One is a bunch of white plastic teacups with pink hearts lining the saucers. Then there's a ceramic olive green set—that one is really mine. It was a present for Three Kings Day when I was nine. After I'd seen Disney's *Mulan* six or seven times, I'd kept asking for some of those funny teacups with no handles. But I never used the set. Not even once. It's a cold hard fact that it just sat in one corner of my room collecting dust. So last year, my sister claimed the tea set as hers, saying, "They're almost like the cups at Chloe's house. Even though these ones are really Chinese, not Japanese."

And now I'm stuck at a pretend tea ceremony for the hundredth time, wondering how I can make this go-round any fun. "Aha!" I point a finger straight into the air. "What if I'm a detective visiting Japan and there's an ancient mystery to be solved?"

Lah clenches both fists and pounds her knees. "No mysteries at Japanese tea parties!" Then she talks like a miniature grown-up about honor and beauty and the eternity of water, stuff she must've heard at Chloe's house.

"But hang about one moment, dear," I say in my best Sherlock Holmes accent. "Might I suggest I'm a super sleuth who's traveled all the way from London to the Orient. Something's afoot in the water and it's stealing all the honor and disrupting the eternal beauty."

Lah jumps up and down, trying to cover my mouth with one teeny hand. "No mysteries! No sloots!"

I squirm out of her grip. "SL-EU-TH-S."

23

My sister's mouth presses into a skinny line. Obviously, she's five seconds from whining all the way down to Mami and Titi Nessa, who are working in the basement studio. Not wanting to get stuck with a lecture and extra chores, I say, "Fine. We'll do it your way."

She points to her doll nestled in a red knit blanket Titi Nessa made. "Unwrap Delilah Juniorette and use the blanket to cover that weird animal on your shirt. No alligators allowed." She's forever changing the rules for Tea Time etiquette.

"Just so you know, this is a lizard on my shirt." Close to losing my patience, I force a smile and drape the blanket over my shoulders.

She skips across the bubble-gum-pink carpet to her American Girl desk and snaps up two more pencils. "Stick these in your hair."

"I'm not putting pencils in my hair." Because there's no way I'm taking off my hat.

Lah tilts her head right and studies me. "You need something nice to make yourself beautiful, Ju."

I can feel my face turning hot and red. "I'm already beautiful," I say calmly. Even though part of me wants to yank out those precious pencils stuck in her perfect brown ponytail and dice them in Mami's food processor.

"You'd look bet-ter with th-eee-se," she informs me in the singsong voice I hate.

"Better? You look ri-di-cu-lous!" I snatch up the tray with all the pieces it took her forever to prepare.

"You're spilling the tea!"

"It's pretend." I grit my teeth. "There is no tea."

I storm into the hallway with the tray. Lah chases after, catches one of my arms, and jerks on it. Pottery flies everywhere, something shatters. I skid to a stop. Three teacups land safely on the tan hallway carpet. But tiny pieces of olive green are scattered all over the light blue tile of the bathroom floor.

"Ju! You broke my—"

"It's not *yours*. It's *my* tea set!"

Our mother appears in the doorway. "What's going on?" We both jump. Mami eyes the bathroom floor.

"Ju broke it," Lah whines. Her lower lip juts out and a tear rolls down one cheek. Great. Here come the waterworks.

"It fell when she grabbed my arm," I say, hoping my mother will appreciate my honesty.

"*Ay*, enough! The tea set is mine now."

"But—" Lah and I say in unison, my voice now as whiny as hers.

"Delilah, no tea parties for three days. To your room. *Now.*"

My sister hiccups down the hall to her room.

Mami turns to me. "No computer or phone tonight."

Ugh. So I can't even call Ig like I'd promised.

She lifts the tray and sets it on the counter. "Take off the hat, Justina."

Oh no. She knows.

"But I, uh—" I fiddle with my *coquí* necklace.

25

She props her hands on her hips. "Should I do it for you?"

I pull off my hat. She pats one side of my wild hair, frowning. "Next time, spread Vaseline along your hairline and the dye won't stain your forehead."

Huh? No screaming?

"The spots are fading, at least." She grabs a cotton ball and baby oil from the medicine cabinet. "But it's not like you to take something of mine without permission."

"Sorry." I spot a piece of the broken teacup behind the small white garbage can and wish I could hide there with it. "I was going to buy you another box."

"And you will. Use some of the money from your last birthday." Mami dabs my forehead with an oily cotton ball. "Leave this for a couple hours then rinse it off with my exfoliating face wash."

I nod.

She raises her eyebrows. "Want me to take you to Paquita's Salon and have them dye it blond again?"

"No," I say right away.

"When I was your age I wanted to be blond," she says. "What do you think about that?"

I shrug. "It wouldn't look right on you."

She sighs. "I'll let you tell your father when you're ready."

"Thanks." She's letting me off easy, after all.

"No television for a week, including movie night."

Or not. I frown and click my tongue.

She purses her lips. "I can make it longer."

26

I shake my head.

"Please clean this mess," Mami says before heading downstairs. "And when you're done, check in on your sister."

Right. I forgot. I'm still in charge of Lah until Papi gets home. Some babysitter I am.

CHAPTER FIVE:
BACKSTAGE CLUES

Here it is, lunchtime on Wednesday in the cafetorium, but there's no hint the Seventh-Grade Sleuths are about to start an investigation. Gunther isn't even here. Ig and I are sitting across from each other at one end of a long white folding table. I swallow the last bite of my peanut butter and jelly sandwich on multi-grain bread and take a gulp of orangeade. "So it was all Lah's fault I couldn't call you last night. Right?"

"I guess." He's taking forever to eat some neon-orange ground meat on a bun. Talk about mysteries.

"Lucky you don't have a little sister," I say.

He shrugs. "Older sisters are a pain too."

Sara Baker appears out of nowhere to hover over us like an annoying pink gnat. She eyes three girls studying at the opposite end of the lunch table and clears her throat. "Five minutes." She points across the room to a door on one side of the brand-new stage. "Meet me at that entrance," she says in an exaggerated read-my-lips whisper, as if what she's asking is illegal.

"I think Gunther's getting math tutoring this period," I say.

"Catch him up later." She lowers her voice. "The stage isn't being used right now. Don't miss our window of opportunity."

I roll my eyes. What a drama queen. "Okay, five minutes then."

She glides away like a ballerina, over to the table where a gaggle of her friends applaud her twirling.

Ig stabs his half-eaten bun with a plastic fork. "Since when do you take orders from Sara?"

Not this again. "Aren't you just a little curious?"

"Nope." He crosses his arms. "Got too much on my mind."

"But this is the perfect distraction from the genetics assignment." I pack away my reusable lunch bag. "Come on, we're already down one detective without Gunther. You can take notes."

Ig stares at his workbook, forehead wrinkled. The muscles in his jaw look tense. "I don't want to take notes *or* go backstage *or* help Sara with her stupid little problem!"

One of the girls on the other side of the table glances up from her textbook.

"What're you going to do, then?" I ask, puzzled and a little embarrassed.

"Homework!"

I try to pretend Ig didn't just yell at me in the middle of lunch, because it's more important that he gets his mind off this project. "You can do it later," I whisper.

He throws down his fork. "I'm sick of you bossing me around!"

This time all the girls at the other end of our table and some kids behind Ig turn to stare.

"We're just rehearsing for, um...an oral report." I smile cheerfully, hoping it'll make them go back to ignoring us. I'm surprised when it actually works.

Ig snaps up his workbook. "Don't assume just because you agreed to help, I'll tag along to play secretary." He shoves the book into his backpack and storms out.

I shake my head and toss away the lunch garbage, then grab the mystery casebook and head for the stage. At the door Sara locks onto my wrist and drags me up the steps behind her, through a maze of long black curtains, costume racks, and half-painted scenery flats. We finally stop at a table with a bunch of random stuff set out on it: a pig-snout mask, some huge fake dollars, a purple crown.

I pick up a floppy yellow rubber chicken. "Eew."

"No touching the props!" Sara whips the bird from my hands and plops it back in the same place. She reaches behind the table and slides out a few flat pieces of oddly-shaped light blue foam. Must be the evidence. But I don't see her name, only a machine-printed logo: **DOW Insulation Styrofoam**. Each piece she turns around looks like it's been finger-painted green by a five-year-old. I'm guessing they're supposed to be something that grows in nature—maybe blobby bushes? And sure enough, smack in the middle of every one, someone has carefully gouged out tiny chunks, exposing the blue unpainted foam underneath so that it spells out **SARA**.

"I hid them before anybody saw," she says. "But Ms. Lee asked the set crew to find them. She wants to reuse these shrubs from last year's play for this production."

Aha! They are shrubs. One mystery down. But seriously, I can see why Sara's totally creeped out. What a bizarre and tedious form of graffiti. I mean, who would bother? Maybe only someone with a really serious grudge. Someone possibly armed with very sharp fingernails. Someone possibly...dangerous. So it's time to gather the cold hard facts, even though I'm Holmes without a Watson. "Find anything else near it?"

"Yeah." She plods over to the wastebasket next to the prop table and, from behind it, fishes out a shoebox. "Here." She opens it to reveal a bunch of half-blue, half-green foam scraps. "Most of the pieces were already inside this box. As if someone's been stockpiling the

31

foam bits. But there were loose chunks on the floor, too. Maybe the vandal ran out of time to finish collecting them all. I swept it up myself."

I gawk at her. "You used a broom?"

"Ha ha." She hides the box again, then crosses her arms. "You're so totally hilarious."

I open to a blank page in the casebook. "What are all the ways to get onto the stage?"

Sara points to the opposite side at a pair of double doors with a glowing red exit sign over them. "Those lead to the hallway. Right next to the technician's cage are entries to the dressing rooms." Alongside the fenced-in console with lots of buttons stand two wooden doors, a few feet apart. One says *GIRLS*. The other, *BOYS*. "But all of those doors are kept locked except during rehearsals. The only entrance open during the day is the one from the cafetorium."

I rub my chin. "Who painted the scenery, the local daycare?"

"Very funny." She tosses long straight auburn hair over one shoulder. "Seth Bernstein and Gunther Corrie."

"Wait a minute. Gunther's on crew?" Why don't I know this already?

"He was last year. And he's on the list this year too, but only shows up when he feels like it." She slides the foam back behind the prop table.

"Where exactly did you discover the evidence?"

"Leaning over there." She points to the wall behind me. I step closer to inspect. Just a plain brick wall,

32

painted black. Out of the corner of one eye I spot something tucked behind yet another curtain. An almost-empty costume rack. Which I wouldn't have noticed at all except for a huge light-pink skirt so poufy it made the curtain bulge out. The fabric covers several hoops that shape it into an enormous bell.

"Here's my costume." Sara wheels out the squeaky rack and holds up the skirt. "Ms. Lee had me wear it while we learned the choreography, and I landed right on my butt. That cannot happen during the show. I'd just die." She drags the curtain back to hide the rack again. "Know what I don't get? On stage I wear ridiculous outfits because of the characters I play. But most days *you* come to school wearing something strange for no reason. Like those weird capris you've got on now." She points to my patchwork bloomers.

"They're hand-made." I grit my teeth. "One-of-a-kind."

She laughs right in my face. "You realize what century we're living in, right?"

I tap one foot on the glossy stage floor. "You want my help or not?"

She holds back the giggling, but still has this goofy smile. "Ever consider a makeover?"

I roll my eyes and let my head fall back. "No. Not ever." My hat falls to the ground before I can catch it.

Sara gawks as if a mangy dog has climbed up to sit on my head. "Whoa. No way. What happened?"

I snatch up the hat and dust it off, grateful that Mami's baby oil trick worked. At least there are no brown splotches on my forehead anymore. "Tried a new look."

She grabs my arm as if this is a medical emergency. "Oh my goodness. My sister Megan can fix the color. Even style your hair stick-straight. I mean, if you want to try a better new look."

She stares intently. Obviously with no clue about what insults she's just spewed. "Don't. Need. A makeover. And I'll only do the sleuth thing if you promise not to bring up the M-word ever again."

Sara considers it. "Fine."

"I'll need a list of the cast and crew," I add. "And a rehearsal schedule."

"No problem. Hey, wasn't Ig going to join you? What happened?"

I turn away and shrug like I don't really care. "Don't know."

And you know what? It turns out that's the cold, hard truth.

CLUES:

– Vandalism occurred backstage on or before audition day

– Daytime access to stage only through cafetorium

– Doors to hallway and dressing rooms unlocked during rehearsal only

– Current possible suspects: cast & crew

- Vandal left foam bits @ scene (Had to leave quickly?)

TO DO:

- Get cast & crew list and rehearsal schedule from Sara
- Interview them all
- Uncover possible motives.

THROWBACK: THIRD GRADE
WHO WORE THIS?

When I was eight I wasn't allowed to go up to the attic alone. Mami always went with me. One of the times I ventured up the narrow steps, I was lugging poster board for a family tree project. I'd drawn sprawling branches, each carefully labeled with names and dates of birth. There were a lot more limbs on her side since she had three siblings, and Papi was an only child. My mother and I were on a mission to find pictures of family members to match each name.

The stash of old, faded photos – some black and white with curled, yellowing edges – smelled musty like the antique trunk she kept them in. "This'll be yours one day," she said, after opening the creaky chest. It had always been passed down to the first-born in Mami's family, for generations.

With one finger I traced the line on the poster board of all the names who'd owned the heirloom trunk. Mami, Abuela Irmita, and my great-grandfather, Polanco. My mother was quick to pick out a photo of my grandmother as a bride. Then one of my great-grandfather smoking a pipe. Even in the black and white images I could tell their coloring was exactly like Mami's: sun-kissed skin, deep dark eyes, and brown hair.

In a cloth pocket on the back wall of the trunk, a shiny bit of metal peeked out. I tugged at the silvery piece and out had popped a pendant with a strange symbol on it — a vertical line with a pair of eyes and four legs. "Cool."

Mami peered up from the stack of photo albums in her lap and froze. "Oh." She'd glanced at the back of the trunk where the charm had been hidden and her expression softened. "That's the Taino symbol for the coquí.*"*

Of course. The Tainos were natives of Puerto Rico. I examined the charm and recognized the symbol as the little island frog named for its song: coh-KEE! coh-KEE!

I scanned the pictures, searching for a woman wearing the pendant. "Who'd it belong to?"

"Your grandmother." Mami took a deep breath then smiled. "Your Abuelita...on your father's side."

"Can I keep it?" She'd nodded and helped me fasten the chain around my neck.

I ran my fingers over the cold metal. "It can be passed down, too. Just like the trunk."

Mami blinked hard, and then she'd looked away. "Your grandmother would've liked that."

Somehow, even then, the little silver coquí *had felt like it was already mine.*

CHAPTER SIX:
TITI NESSA'S OPINION

I've had a few days to mull over the clues Sara
showed me. But since she hasn't even given me the
cast list yet, there's not much investigating I can do.
Besides, it's Saturday. That means I should get cracking
on my genetics assignment.

The burnt-plastic hot glue smell hits me on the way
downstairs into the basement studio. Mami's gluing
bottle caps onto a jewelry box. My aunt glances up from
the sewing machine, a straight pin clamped between
her lips.

I flop onto a stool next to tall shelves that overflow
with baskets, fabric and trim. I run a hand across
several yards of soft cotton with a daisy print.

"Seriously, Titi. You're going to swallow one of those pins someday."

"Your aunt's been doing that since before you were born," Mami says. "She's not going to stop now."

Titi Nessa takes the pin from her mouth and stabs the pattern of lacy material lying on the huge worktable in front of her. Her piercing green eyes are bright against her mocha skin. She wears her black hair in short curls, tight against her head. "Guess you really like that hat I made for you." She gestures at my head.

Mami chuckles. "Why not show your aunt the reason for your fashion statement?"

"Don't laugh." I playfully toss a ball of yarn in my mother's direction.

"What happened?" Titi Nessa asks. "Did you cut all your hair off?"

"No." I sigh and finally remove the hat.

"Ay." She raises her eyebrows. "Well, that's different. Are you becoming a master of disguise like a character in one of those mysteries you like?"

"No. Just wanted to see what I look like with brown hair."

Titi glances at my mother. "You knew about this?"

"I figured it out when a box of dye went missing," Mami says. "Anyway, I thought about going blond in high school, remember? Me, I dreamed of being Malibu Barbie."

"But you never actually changed your hair color, Alana." My aunt seems really serious about some stupid little hair dye experiment.

I pick a piece of lint off the hat. "It looks that bad, Titi?"

She smiles at me. "I just think you look great with your natural color, *m'ija*."

"I agree," my mother says. "But she wants to keep it. Now she just has to show her father."

Titi frowns. "He doesn't know?"

"Not yet." I try shoving the hair back in the hat but it keeps escaping. "Ma, I came down to find out if you know about any hereditary conditions that run in our family."

"What?" She turns to me, squinting. "Why do you ask?"

"We're learning about genetics," I say. "Supposed to find out as much as we can about the genes we've inherited."

"I see. But...didn't you already do this in third grade?" She sets the glue gun on the table. "I helped you make that family tree."

"This isn't for a family tree, Ma." I sigh. "More like calculating what our chances are of getting a bunch of horrible diseases based on our ancestry. You know, like heart disease, diabetes, cancer."

My aunt clicks her tongue. "Now that's one depressing project."

"More than depressing," Mami says. "It's an invasion of privacy. Frankly, I'm surprised it's allowed. Who assigned this?"

"Mrs. Mollick."

"Hmm." She crosses her arms. "I'll call her."

Obviously she doesn't understand how important the project is. "It's twenty-five percent of my grade for the semester." I slide my *coquí* charm back and forth on its chain. Why get so upset about a simple school assignment?

"Stop playing with that necklace," Mami yells. "You're going to break it."

Titi Nessa clears her throat. "Shouldn't you maybe discuss the project when Oscar's home? Then you can all come to an agreement once everyone's had their say."

Here's the thing about my aunt. Besides the Craft-e-Shop, she also works full time as a high school guidance counselor. So even though Titi doesn't have her own kids, sometimes she likes to offer my mother professional advice about dealing with me and Lah.

"Don't lecture me about parenting, Nessa."

They both scowl then and go back to work without saying another word.

That leaves me to hunt down the cold hard facts about family history on my own. But this detective business is beginning to feel less like some fun, intriguing puzzle that needs to be solved and more like a punishment.

41

CHAPTER SEVEN:
CLUES IN THE ATTIC

I leave Mami and Titi hard at work in the basement. The rest of the house is empty. Papi's at work. Lah is over at Chloe's. I climb our dark and narrow staircase, making a creak with each step, then yank the hanging cord for the attic's single bulb. It shines on a million specks of dust floating in slow motion. I step over a rowing machine and almost fall into a three-foot tall plastic Rudolph on my way back to the trunk.

I'm guessing Mami keeps old family documents in here. If so, I should be able to find what I need for the genetics project pretty easily. I use both hands to pry open the large metal latch, which sticks. Finally it snaps open, sending a puff of dust into the musty air.

Coughing, I lug out stacks of photo albums, then a high school yearbook.

I run a hand over the bumpy lettering on its smooth, glossy cover.

Central Avenue High School
"A Time To Remember"

Mami's told me and Lah stories about her high school days. How she'd come to the mainland from Puerto Rico when she was fourteen. And how the kids made fun of her accent even though she got top grades on English essays. I flip through the yearbook to find her picture: Long hair, poufy on top. Tan face that makes her stand out from the other students on the page. Most have skin as light as mine.

I lay the yearbook back on the bottom of the trunk. It feels crazy to realize it was four whole years ago Mami and I were up here searching for pictures for the family tree project. Back when I'd found my grandmother's *coquí* necklace.

Of course! I forgot to check the back pocket of the trunk. I slip a hand into the flap sewn flat against the inside rear of the trunk, afraid I might run into a spider web.

All I find is a stack of recipe cards tied together with a thin white string. Flan, rum cake, *dulce de leche*, rice pudding, *tembleque*, pumpkin bread. Strange. Why would Mami keep recipes tucked away up where she can't use them? The fanciest she's ever gotten with baking dessert is oatmeal chocolate-chip cookies. On the bottom of the pile there's a small white envelope addressed to my mother. *W. D. MARTIN* is written in scratchy blue letters above the return address.

Just then Mami calls out something all the way from the first floor. Up here I can't hear what it is. But if she sees me in the attic, she'll know I'm searching for family information for my project. I shove the envelope back in the trunk and quickly shut the lid. I leap over the rowing machine and rush back down the narrow steps, only to look back and notice the attic light's still on.

"You hear me, *niña?* I asked you a question," she yells, still one floor beneath me. But she's making her way up to the second floor hallway. Soon she'll notice the attic light and know I've been up there.

Thank goodness the phone rings just then and she answers it. "Hello...oh, hi, Anna. I hope Delilah's behaving herself...sure, she can spend the night...I'll drop off a bag..." Her voice grows fainter as she wanders back down to the first floor. I dash up the attic stairs, two at a time, yank the string for the light then race back to the second floor. Slumped against the wall in the hallway, I pant, trying to catch my breath.

"W. D. Martin," I whisper.

Who is that? And why would Mami hide the envelope with a stack of old recipes?

I run into my room and yank out my casebook. Flipping to a page in the back I write all I remember seeing.

CLUES IN THE ATTIC:

- W. D. Martin
- State: CT (Connecticut)
- Envelope of dessert recipes

While Mami goes to drop off Lah's overnight bag at Chloe's, I sneak into Papi's home office with my casebook and search the Internet for W. D. MARTIN. Over three million listings pop up. I search again, this time adding Connecticut. I dig my toes into the light brown carpeting and scan the results. Click through a couple scrolls. There's a listing for a detective in Mylesburg, Connecticut, named W. D. Martin. The link leads to a website. It shows a picture of a woman with chin-length red hair, wearing a dark green suit.

W. D. Martin, Private Detective
Get answers to your questions or you don't pay!

"Where's the hat?" Titi says from the doorway behind me.

I stifle a gasp and minimize the screen, then swivel slowly in the chair to face her. "In my, um, room." I'm

45

pretty sure it's not, though. It must've fallen off in the attic, but I can't tell her that.

"Hey." My aunt studies a large clay object lying on the shelf of Papi's computer desk. "Your father's had this a while."

"A couple years." I was so proud when I made the sculpture in art class two years ago and wrapped it up as a gift for Papi's birthday. By now I can admit it looks like a glazed black lump of tar. "It's supposed to be the Maltese Falcon from the Humphrey Bogart movie."

She laughs. "You're kidding, right?"

In the film, all these people search for a priceless statue that turns out to be a fake. "Yeah. Looks more like a crooked pigeon," I say. "But Papi claims it's perfect the way it is."

"*Bueno*, he must mean that, since he displays it so proudly."

I shrug. "I guess."

"Abuela Irma might be able to help you with some of the info you need," Titi says.

"Great." I slump back into the chair. "If I even do the project."

"I'm sure your mother will come around. I'll be in the basement if you need me." Her footsteps are light on the stairs as she heads back down.

I stare at the lady detective on the screen, trying to understand all that's happened. Ma freaking out about my project. This strange clue in the attic. A red-haired

46

mystery woman. How I wish I could talk to Ig about all this.

Through the window, I see it's getting dark out. Wonder if Ig's on his way to the observatory right now. If only I was with him at this moment, thinking about the craters on the moon instead of—

The keyboard vibrates on the desk as the garage door goes up and rattles down again. That was quick. Mami got home sooner than I expected. Or is it Papi finally home from work? Either way, I'm not supposed to be online when they're not here unless it's for schoolwork. My shaking fingers type the link to my school's HOMEWORK HELP site and click the little pencil icon. My heart races as Papi's heavy footsteps climb the garage stairs.

"Justina?" He calls, as he enters the room. "Oh! You dyed your hair?"

Ay. I forgot. My hands shoot up to cover my head. "Yeah, I...um, yeah."

He looks at it for a moment, then asks quietly, "Why?"

Should I say, Because this stupid assignment has me feeling even more like a freak in my own family? "Oh, you know. Thought I'd see what darker hair looked like." I turn away and face the computer screen. "Mami's okay with it. Besides, you never said I wasn't allowed to."

"Hmm." He shifts his weight. "I suppose you're right." But I can feel him there, still behind me, waiting for – what?

At last, he sighs and leaves the room.

I click back to the page with W. D. Martin, staring at her image as if it could speak and answer my questions. Like: What's in that envelope, and why would my parents hide it? Why did my mother hire a private detective? That is, if it's the same mysterious W. D. Martin as on the return address.

The Strange Case of the Backstage Vandal is one thing. But the Secret Identity of W. D. Martin is a mystery I suddenly wish didn't exist.

CHAPTER EIGHT:
THE SOLO SLEUTH

Another Monday, another lonely lunch period in the cafetorium. The three girls across the table are silent, faces buried in books. I've been staring at the same math problem for fifteen minutes. It's just impossible to focus on homework. I keep imagining sneaking back up into the attic to get that mysterious envelope.

I glance at the other end of the long lunch table. Ig is sitting down there by himself, listening to an iPod, eyes squeezed shut, chin propped on one fist. The hood of his blue sweatshirt is pulled up.

I rub my nose. The air in here smells like a strange mix of bologna, mustard, and...nail polish? Sure enough, two rows away Sara and Ayesha Malloy are busy painting designs on their arms with a bottle of nail polish and its tiny brush.

Since I can't concentrate on homework, why not do some investigating on Sara's case? Though with Ig ignoring me, and Gunther nowhere to be found, I'm the solo sleuth. Again.

I sigh and take out my investigation notes about the school play. I've taped the Seriousland cast and crew list (that is, my suspect list) onto one of the pages of the casebook. I've already crossed off Sara's name. So it looks like this:

SERIOUSLAND

CAST LIST:
Lady Luciana— ~~Sara Baker~~
Sir Serious—Franklin Diaz
The Jester—Ayesha Malloy
The Servant—Janine Petite
The Beggar—Elizabeth Moore
The Prince—Raj Gupta
Female Understudy—Nina Minchi
Male Understudy—Seth Bernstein

Set Construction/Tech Crew:
Seth Bernstein, Gunther Corrie, Nina Minchi, Elijah Roberts

Director and Choreographer: Erica Lee
Stage Manager, Sound and Light Designer: Don Vincent
Costume Designer: Betty Unger
Wardrobe Assistant: Nina Minchi

Rehearsal: Mon-Fri, 3:00-5:00pm
Tech Crew: Mon-Fri, 5:15-6:30pm
No food or drinks allowed in dressing rooms or stage areas!!!

First thing that stands out is the fifteen-minute break between rehearsal and crew call. An obvious opportunity. The stage crew has easiest access to the scenery. It makes sense to question them first. I catch up to Elijah Roberts as he's setting his tray on the brand-new conveyor belt. "Elijah! Set crew, right?"

"*You* wanna *join?*" He stares at me wide-eyed.

I try not to laugh, picturing myself handling a saw or an electric drill. "No. I'm doing, um, a report on backstage life. You know, for extra credit." Everyone knows white lies are allowed during an investigation, to draw out the potential suspects. That's when they always let some important detail slip out.

"*Awesome* idea for a project!"

Whoa. This kid gets excited about anything. Maybe he ought to be on stage performing, not backstage building the set. "Did you audition?" I ask, as if it's no big deal.

He shakes his head. "No way. I get *crazy* stage fright. Besides, Ms. Lee picked the best cast. Wait'll you see the play. They're *amazing!*"

"Everyone else on crew thinks so?"

"Yep." He tilts his head. "Except...well, Nina *really* wanted the role of Lady Luciana. The other day she made a joke about how she'd be *cuter* than Sara in that crazy costume. Mr. Vincent said it was going against *backstage code*, talking like that."

So Nina Minchi, the female understudy, had her sights set on Sara's part. Definitely a Person of Interest. "What do the others think about her comment?"

Elijah scratches at his dark brown skin. "O.M.G. We ignore her. All she does is brag: *'I* study acting with Broadway professionals...*I* stay after school to help Mrs. Unger create the costumes...*I* can run the sound and light boards by myself...in my *sleep...UNDERWATER!'*"

I raise my eyebrows at him. "So Nina helps make the costumes?"

He nods so hard it's got to be hurting his neck. "Her mom's a costume designer as, like, her *career.* So let's just say Nina's, um, a little *nuts* about the costumes being *authentic.* You should've heard her blabbing about that stupid hoop *skirt.*"

Okay. This seems promising. What if Nina knows it'll be impossible to do the dance numbers in that authentic hoop skirt? Maybe she secretly wants Sara to injure herself. If the lead can't perform, Nina would replace her in the role of Lady Luciana.

Exactly the kind of investigative lead I've been hoping for.

I smile at Elijah. "Hey, thanks."

"Sure thing." He beams back. "Oh, and Ju? *Love* the dye job!"

I shoot him a thumbs-up. Back at the table, I open the casebook, cross off Elijah's name from the suspect list, and take notes on what I've learned so far:

ELIJAH: Interviewed, not a current suspect
- On set crew
- No interest in performing (stage fright)
- Really excited about the production

NINA: *Person of interest/current lead suspect*
- Female understudy, also on set crew and wardrobe mistress
- Helped make dress (thinks she'd be cuter than Sara in L.L.'s costume)

A loud clanging of metal from the kitchen area makes me jump in my seat. My messenger bag goes

53

flying. When I lean over to pick up loose papers, Ig's staring at me. For a second, it seems like he might come over to help. Instead, he squeezes his eyes shut again, tighter. The bell rings. I stay seated. But Ig takes the long way around, trudging past the last table near the edge of the stage.

Sara skips over. "Saw you talking to Elijah. Any news?"

I shake my head. "No breaks in the case yet. What do you know about Nina Minchi?"

She rolls her eyes. "Lots of attitude for such a tiny girl." Her eyes widen, then narrow. "Oh! So it's her?"

"Nothing conclusive yet." I take out my subject folders from the messenger bag. "Just wanted your opinion on Nina, is all."

"Find out soon, okay? The stress is really affecting my rehearsal process." She slinks off dramatically.

"Diva," I mutter under my breath. Nina's not the only one with too much attitude.

Lunch periods are done for the day. I stay behind after the cafetorium clears out. Next is study hall so it's not like I'm missing any classes. One of the sheets that fell out of my bag is still on the floor. When I try to pick it up the paper's stuck to something greenish and it tears in two. Mrs. Mollick's genetics assignment.

"Ay." I rip the paper in half. And in half and in half and—

"Tryin' to make my job harder, young lady?" Alfred, the maintenance man says. He's sweeping up a spilled juice box a few feet away, blue eyes focused on the torn bits covering the floor like confetti.

"Oh." I hadn't realized what a mess I was creating. "Oh gosh. Sorry."

"Hmph." He empties the dustpan. "Gonna be late for class."

"It's just study hall."

"That all?" He raises his eyebrows. "I'll start at the other end."

"Thanks. I'll be done real soon."

I re-organize my folders: Earth Science, English, Health Studies, Pre-Algebra, U.S. History. There's another clanging of metal followed by a long, grating screech. I turn to see Alfred yanking down the big metal gate for the kitchen, securing the locks. It hits me now: he's a possible witness! Maybe he didn't see the incident happen, but he must've come across evidence.

"Hey, Alfred. When do you clean up backstage?"

He shakes his head. "Ms. Lee takes over that cleaning duty whenever there's a play. Been that way ever since I threw away a bag of fake garbage a couple years back." He laughs. "A prop. Looked like the real thing to me."

I try to smile even though I actually want to cry. Something about this huge, empty, echoing cafetorium makes me feel lonely.

He rests both palms on the tip of the broom handle. "Hey. You okay, kiddo?"

"Yeah." I nod. "Thanks for not kicking me out." I slip the folders back into my bag.

"Sure thing." He shrugs and goes back to sweeping.

I start to clean the paper scattered over the gray tiles, but he flaps a hand at the mess. "Don't worry about that. I got it."

As he sweeps the pile into a smaller and smaller mound, I get a sinking feeling in the pit of my stomach. Because it's a cold hard fact that my friendship with Ig is just like that paper—all in pieces. Maybe even about to be trashed.

THROWBACK: SECOND GRADE
WHERE I'M FROM

When your parents are born on a faraway island, you grow up feeling like you own a little bit of it. Like it's where you're from, too.

Sara asked me once, back when we were in Mr. Shah's second grade class, "How can you be from two places?"

To explain, I'd pointed to two spots on the globe, keeping my pointer finger on New Jersey. "I was born here. But my parents were born there." My pinky was planted on a green speck surrounded by blue.

"An island?" She frowned.

"Puerto Rico," I said, smiling, head held high.

Ig pointed to an island near Florida shaped like a vacuum cleaner. "My parents were born there." He glanced up to see Sara's reaction, but she'd already wandered away.

We'd looked at each other and shrugged, then turned back to the globe. Ig tried to cover Cuba with his entire thumb. I used the tip of my pointer finger to block out Puerto Rico.

"Where you're from is way bigger than where I'm from," I said at last.

He'd nodded and looked thoughtful. "Yeah."

With Ig it was always like that. I never had to explain stuff. He'd always understood.

CHAPTER NINE:
THE UNDERSTUDY OR THE PRINCE?

The halls are filled with students going through the usual after-school routine. I pop my head into the sewing classroom. Its tall windows overlook the blacktop behind the school. Mrs. Unger isn't around, but Nina Minchi is hard at work stitching arcs of purple and green felt into a curved, pointed cone. An easel in front of her holds a pattern with some penciled-in measurements under the heading:

JESTER'S HAT (Actor: Ayesha Malloy)

The clean scent of freshly-ironed cotton reminds me of when I took sewing in this room last year. I'd figured to be a natural since I'd watched Mami and Titi Nessa stitch all those clothes and household items for their online store. But I'd had all kinds of trouble just making a simple, square pillow.

The whirring of the machine stops. Nina turns away and snatches another hook-shaped piece of felt off a tall wooden cutting table. *"Orange?"* she groans, with a sour expression. As if the bright pumpkin color was really the exact shade of dog poop.

I laugh. "What's the matter? Not Ayesha's best color?"

"Aaaaahh!" Nina jumps and whirls in her seat to face me. "Geez, you scared the stuffing out of me."

"Sorry." I take the piece of material from her hand and hold it up to catch the sunlight beaming in through the ceiling-high windows. "Hmm, I like it."

"You would." She glances at a clipboard and sighs. "I told Mrs. Unger we needed to use Mardi Gras colors for the Jester. Purple, green, and *gold.* Not freaking orange." She tosses the clipboard onto the table. "She'll be back in ten minutes, by the way."

"Oh, good. I'll wait, then." Perfect. Let her believe I'm here for the teacher. A cold hard fact: it's best when your number-one suspect doesn't even realize she's being questioned.

I slump into a worn chair in front of bins of thread and scissors.

Nina touches my aquamarine bracelet. "Nice beadwork. Pretty color, too."

"Thanks," I say. "My aunt made it for me."

"Did a good job." She shifts her gaze to my silver necklace. "And I like the shape of your charm."

"Thanks." Now's not the time for a round of compliments, though. I need to steer this conversation toward Nina and the play. "You know, probably no one in the audience would notice if you used orange instead of gold."

"But I'd notice." She fishes a pack of gum from her tiny lilac, box-shaped purse. "So would my mom. She designs for professional theaters and colleges. She'd never use orange as a Mardi Gras color." She pops hot-pink gum into her mouth.

I take a piece when she offers, then practically choke on the strong, sour-watermelon taste. Gasping, I grab a water bottle from my messenger bag and take a bunch of gulps. "Can't designers get away with cheating on certain things for a play?" I cough, eyes watering. "I mean, with the distance of the audience, and all."

She frowns. "How do you cheat on color?"

"Hmm. Good point." Looks like I'll need a more direct approach. "So what's Sara Baker wearing?"

Nina smiles. "A hoop skirt the color of a cherry blossom and a beige corset with puffed magenta sleeves. Mrs. Unger let me help sew the bottom half. At first, she was just going to use layers of petticoats." She rolls her eyes. "But I convinced her to add a plastic hoop to make it more authentic."

"Must be hard to dance in though."

Nina blinks, chomping away at her gum, staring at me blankly.

"I mean, maybe Mrs. Unger thought the hoop might get in Sara's way. Trip her up while she was, you know, dancing or whatever."

Nina sniffs as she adjusts the red headband holding back her stick-straight, jet-black hair. "Real actresses learn how to work with whatever costume they're given." She marches over to the upright steam iron and flicks it on with force.

She definitely appears to be a jealous understudy— one who's trying to keep the leading lady from doing a good job with a part she wanted to play herself. So there's motive. But even if all this talk of authentic costumes is a cover for creating a hazardous dress on purpose, it doesn't prove she's the scenery vandal. Besides, I'm not sure she had the opportunity. "Hmm, Mrs. Unger is still not back. Does she leave you alone here a lot?"

Nina shrugs. "She always has to run over to the new kitchen classroom."

One of the school's renovations is a brand new, state-of-the-art cooking room on the far end of the seventh-grade annex. That's cool for us since it leaves the hallway smelling like cookies or brownies every afternoon. But poor Mrs. Unger is always running back and forth now in her long, flowery dresses, to teach one class or another, always in more of a rush than the students.

This means Nina would've had time to sneak backstage without her ever knowing she'd left the room. "Wow. You're the female understudy, the wardrobe assistant, and on tech crew, too? Must get tiring."

Nina hangs a ruffled shirt from a tall hook attached to the steamer. "I never have all three in one day. Understudy rehearsal's only once a week. I do have to skip crew when they're working on the foam scenery, though."

"Why's that?"

"I'm allergic to Styrofoam." She takes hold of the steam iron just as a gush of moist heat starts flowing from one end of the long hose. "Can't go near any kind of petroleum-based products or my throat starts closing up." She bugs out her eyes and gives a high, breathy wheeze to demonstrate.

"Oh." *Ay.* So there goes that theory.

I spit the sour, sugary wad of gum into a nearby trashcan and head for the door. "Know what? I can catch up with Mrs. Unger tomorrow." I smile at Nina. "Good luck finding gold."

She scrunches her face and stares at me. "Huh?"

"The Mardi Gras colors."

"Oh, right." She eyes the piece of felt on her sewing station again, frowning, shaking her head in disgust. "Orange."

***

The librarian is busy scanning books behind the check-out desk when I enter. "Hello Justina," he says between beeps of the scanner.

I wave to him on my way to the secret spot back in the alcove. Gunther's already there, lying on his stomach doing math homework. I collapse onto a stool next to him. "I don't think Ig's coming today."

"Noticed you giving him the silent treatment." He closes his math book.

"Nope. Other way around."

He raises his eyebrows. "Didn't know Soto was capable of that."

"I hear you're on set crew," I say, trying not to sound suspicious. "Why's it all so hush-hush?"

"Don't want my father finding out. He says drama club's for girls."

As strange as his excuse sounds, I believe Gunther. It was the same with our mystery club—his dad couldn't find out. For a second, I consider telling him what Papi told me. How, in Shakespeare's time, all the roles were played by men since woman weren't allowed to be actors. But it probably wouldn't help. And anyhow, there are more important things to discuss. "Have you checked out the evidence?"

He nods. "Pretty weird. Especially since I helped paint the scenery last year."

If Gunther were guilty, he wouldn't admit to that. Further proof that he's innocent.

"Can you think of anyone who comes early to crew call?"

"Just Gupta."

Strange. I thought Raj Gupta had a role in the play. I take out the case notebook and scan the cast list. Yeah, that's his name, all right. "But Raj is playing the prince. How's he on crew?"

"He's not, officially. But he stays after, to help."

I dig deep in my bag for a pen. "Does he have something against Sara?"

"Against her?" Gunther snorts. "He's been crushing on the Diva since summer break."

"Hey, this is a great lead!" I grip his arm and smile. "Tomorrow we'll go backstage before rehearsal starts, to study the evidence."

"Uh, but...people might get there early and—"

"See us together?" I let go of him. "I see. So you're only my friend in this corner."

He shakes his head. "It's not like that, Feliciano."

"Yeah." I stand. "Right." I grab my bag and rush out of the library. Gunther can find some other mystery to solve, for all I care.

At my locker, I toss the books I need next into the messenger bag and slam the thin, metal door shut. Then slide down to sit on the floor, clutching the casebook. I rub my *coquí* charm, trying to focus on the mystery. Seth Bernstein is the only crew member left to investigate. Then it's on to the actors. Starting with the one who has a big-time crush on the leading lady. Mister Raj Gupta. I open the casebook, first to the suspect list.

SERIOUSLAND

<u>CAST LIST</u>:
~~*Lady Luciana*—Sara Baker~~
Sir Serious—Franklin Diaz
The Jester—Ayesha Malloy
The Servant—Janine Petite
The Beggar—Elizabeth Moore
The Prince—Raj Gupta
~~Female Understudy—Nina Minchi~~
Male Understudy—Seth Bernstein

Set Construction/Tech Crew:
Seth Bernstein, ~~Gunther Corrie, Nina Minchi, Elijah Roberts~~

Then I take notes.

NINA: ~~*Person of interest/current lead suspect*~~, interviewed, ruled out
- Female understudy, also on set crew and wardrobe mistress

66

- Helped make dress (thinks she'd be cuter than Sara in L.L.'s costume)
- Allergic to Styrofoam

GUNTHER: Investigator, not a current suspect
- On set crew (doesn't want dad to find out)

RAJ: *Person of interest/current lead suspect*
- Plays "The Prince"
- Unofficially on set crew
- Has crush on Sara

CHAPTER TEN:
FUNTASTIC FORUM

It's the first Saturday since summer that Papi isn't working and we're on our way to the Funtastic Forum, an indoor amusement park where I had my tenth birthday party.

"How many minutes till we get the balls and clubs?" Lah keeps screaming, even though I'm right next to her in the backseat of our family's mini-van.

I glare. "Would you stop with the how many, how many, how many?"

It's hard to block her out, but I'm trying to focus on the casebook open on my lap. This past week, I knocked two people off the suspect list. First I tracked down Seth Bernstein in the hallway between classes. Turns out he's head of the stage crew and was frantically searching for the old fake shrubs ever since Ms. Lee mentioned wanting to use them again for this year's production. He actually jumped for joy when I showed him where they were hidden. Of course, I slid one fake bush even further back behind the storage cabinet to keep as evidence in the ongoing investigation. And then there's Liz Moore, who didn't even know insulation foam board was used to build the scenery—*Wouldn't foam be, um, totally soft and flimsy?*—she'd asked while we were both washing our hands in the bathroom. Clueless. I had hoped to question Raj Gupta in gym class, but the boys and girls were split up the entire week. I've updated the suspect list based on all the new info.

SERIOUSLAND

<u>CAST LIST:</u>
Lady Luciana—~~Sara Baker~~
Sir Serious—Franklin Diaz
The Jester—Ayesha Malloy
The Servant—Janine Petite
~~*The Beggar*—Elizabeth Moore~~
The Prince—Raj Gupta
~~Female Understudy—Nina Minchi~~
~~Male Understudy—Seth Bernstein~~

Set Construction/Tech Crew:
~~Seth Bernstein, Gunther Corrie, Nina Minchi,~~
~~Elijah Roberts~~

SETH: Interviewed, not a current suspect
- Male understudy, head of set crew
- In charge of storing set and props
- Going to fix the scenery

LIZ: Interviewed, not a current suspect
- Plays "The Beggar"
- Too clueless about actual building materials to destroy set

"Hey. What's that?" Lah tries to lean over to see what I'm doing, but the seat belt doesn't let her get far.

"None of your business." I slap the notebook shut and slide it into my messenger bag. Then, to distract her, I gasp, "Hey, look!" We're pulling into the parking lot next to the glass building. I point to the enormous waterfall that's part of the eighteenth hole of the mini golf course.

Lah tosses Delilah Juniorette into the air, then catches and squeezes her tight. "Yay! Yay! We're here!"

* * *

Inside the Funtastic Forum, beneath its enormous glass roof, the bright green carpet covering the entire mini golf area slowly darkens as the sun hides behind gray clouds.

At the seventh hole, Lah swings her club and completely misses the ball. "Oops. That one doesn't count."

By now I've lost track of how many do-overs my sister's had. My theory is she's missing the ball on purpose so she can spend extra time wandering around underneath the giant giraffe, her favorite.

"Has Mrs. Mollick mentioned anything about the email I sent her?" Mami asks.

Papi frowns. "I thought we were going to discuss it further before you contacted the teacher."

My mother props her fists on her hips. "Justina shouldn't be required to share private family matters with her entire class!"

Lah swings the club and misses again. "Oops. That one doesn't count, too."

Even though it's the last thing I want to talk about right now, I can't stand by and say nothing. "But I told you. It counts as twenty-five percent of my grade. Plus, it's for the Fall Festival."

"*Ay*, that's absurd." Mami's face is red, which means she's getting worked up.

Papi throws his arms out, palms up. "What're you going to do, take her out of the whole festival?" He accidentally smacks his club against a fake tree.

The thump startles Lah. She flinches, but finally makes contact with the ball. It bounces off one of the giraffe's spotted legs. "Oops. That one doesn't count, too."

"Of course we're not going to pull her out of the festival. Not unless..." My mother takes a deep breath and leans against the top of a giant pink and purple-striped mushroom. "Let's see what Mrs. Mollick says."

Papi stares. "You're willing to put your daughter's grades on the line? Justina's schoolwork is the priority here!"

Mami folds her arms. "It's a matter of principle, Oscar."

"Oh really? Whose?"

She sighs. "Our *family's*."

"Well, I don't agree." He shakes his head.

Mami grips her purse, one she made out of hemp and bamboo, so hard her knuckles look almost white. "I'll just wait in the lobby." She struts away back up the walkway alongside the first section of the course.

"Yay! I got seven!" Lah yells, and runs back underneath the giraffe. Then she sees Mami's leaving. "Hey. Where's she going?"

"Your mother isn't playing anymore," Papi mutters.

Lah tilts her head up to look at him. "She sick?"

A few high school kids standing behind us are shuffling and whispering. One asks, "Uh, you guys playing or not?"

My father pulls us aside. "Sorry. Go on ahead."

72

Lah plops down criss-cross-applesauce on the fake grass, pouting. About Mami. Or having to wait. Or maybe about nothing—sometimes she only pouts to get our parents' attention. But she doesn't have it right now, because Papi's watching me, not her.

"Your mother can't let you ignore school work," he says. "It's not fair to you. Or to your teacher or classmates, for that matter."

Lah tugs on his pant leg. "When is Mami coming back?"

"Don't you listen?" Suddenly, I can't stand the squeaky whine of her little kid voice any longer. "She's not playing anymore. She's mad because of my health homework, so she's waiting in the lobby until we're done."

My sister smacks the golf club against a fake tree, over and over. "No fair! No fair!"

The high school kids are laughing now. "Watch out! That little kid might whack you."

"*Basta*, Delilah," my father yells.

Lah goes for one final hit but I catch the club. "Would. You. Stop."

"Dude, let's skip to the next one," says a guy wearing a baseball cap. "These people are having a family moment." They walk past, under the giraffe. A girl in a red hoodie peeks back at me with raised eyebrows. A look that says, *Hey, I've been there. Lots of luck.*

"Let's go, girls." Papi suddenly seems in a big rush to leave.

73

Lah lies down on the green fake-grass carpet, looking stiff as a board. "No!"

"Delilah Feliciano, you stand up this minute."

My sister sits. "How many minutes until we get home?"

I can't stand it. Light rain smacks the huge glass roof and walls. It's like we're on display, inside some kind of museum exhibit. What would the tour guide say?

Observe here this case, a modern American family: The Felicianos. Two angry parents. One bratty little sister. And the other daughter. The one who doesn't belong. Now isn't she the oddest specimen of all?

CHAPTER ELEVEN:
THE SECRET ENVELOPE

Maybe there was something about yesterday's disastrous trip to the Fantastic Forum that caused the strange dream I had last night.

In it, Detective W. D. Martin was in my bedroom, pinning up prints of photos she'd secretly taken of me. One showed me standing in front of Mami's trunk, holding a live *coquí*. Another image was of me and Ig in the library, hiding behind a fort made of stacked *Sisters Grimm* books. But the weirdest picture was of Gunther, Sara, and me dancing together on stage, doing Broadway choreography, all of us wearing big hoop skirts. A never-ending line-up of photos I kept tearing down. But Detective Martin always had more.

I woke in a sweat, heart jumping like a *coquí* was trapped in my chest.

Creepy as the dream was, it doesn't stop me from sneaking back up to the attic today, while my mother's at the supermarket. Papi's picking up Lah from a morning birthday party. My knit hat is still lying next to the trunk where it landed after I ran out in a big rush the last time. I snatch it up, grab the small white envelope from the trunk, and yank the light cord on my way down the stairs.

Papi's car rumbles into the driveway as I slam the attic door shut.

I rush to lock myself in my room, race across the navy blue carpeting and jump on my bed. I'm about to open the mysterious envelope from W. D. Martin, when there's a knock on the door.

"Go away, Lah."

"I wanna show you my tattoo-oo-oo," my sister sings.

"Later."

"It's not real," she says, scratching at the door like a cat. "It comes off after a bath."

"Go show Papi."

"He already saw." Her tiny fingers wiggle at me through the crack underneath the door. "It's on the back of my hand. See?"

I grit my teeth, shove the envelope into a drawer in my wooden nightstand, and open up. Lah's face is coated with glitter. On the back of one outstretched hand is a dancing pink hippo in a tutu.

I smirk. "Very nice."

"And we did makeup." She props a hand under her chin. "Glitter!"

"Huh. Imagine that. Never would've guessed."

"Look!" She stands on tiptoes. "Look at my cheeks."

"Yeah, I see them." I reach out to close the door right in her glittery, annoying face.

Her eyebrows pop up like twin question marks. "Wanna play Tea Time?"

"No. I need to do homework."

The electric garage door opens, making the floor vibrate. Mami's home from the supermarket, too. Now she'll expect us both downstairs to help unload and put away groceries. Lah's Tea Time will have to wait. And so will the mystery envelope in my nightstand.

Mami unwraps a package of grill-ready shish kebab. Even though there are reddish and yellow leaves scattered across the lawn, today it's warm enough to hang out on the deck in our backyard. The birds above are still singing.

"Get the *adobo*, Oscar," my mother shouts to my father through the sliding door that leads into the kitchen. "I'm giving these the Caribbean touch."

He hands out the container of powdered seasoning.

"Is Car-rib-ee-ah a country?" Lah asks. She's making Delilah Juniorette do back flips along the deck railing.

My parents both laugh as if she's the cutest kid who ever lived.

"There is no such thing as Caribbea." Papi flashes her a smile. "It's the Caribbean Sea."

Her jaw drops. "Eew. Why do you wanna make our food taste like the ocean?"

I roll my eyes. "No, silly. Mami's going to make it taste like the food from the islands *in* the Caribbean Sea."

"Puerto Rico's an island," Lah tells her doll.

"Thank you, Princess Obvious," I mutter.

"Be nice." Papi frowns at me. Then he turns to my sister and smiles again. "You're absolutely right, Delilah."

"It's where our family came from," she says to her toy. "You just can't tell when you look at Ju, because her skin's the wrong color."

Mami yells, "Delilah! You know better than to say such a thing. Puerto Ricans come in—"

My stomach does a somersault.

Lah shouts, "*All* shades!"

My mother shuts her eyes and takes a deep breath. "That's correct."

"But still," my sister squeals. "She doesn't really match us."

"Enough!" Mami drops the *adobo*. It bounces on the deck and lands on its side. The plastic top pops off and

78

seasoning pours out like a mound of sand slowly seeping through the wood slats.

My father picks up the empty container. "I'll get something to—"

"*Déjalo*, Oscar." My mother's hands shake as she sets the kebabs on the grill. "Just let it fall through."

"Enough!" Lah scolds Delilah Juniorette, shaking a finger in the doll's face.

My mother gives my father a stare that seems like a secret signal. Then she quickly opens the sliding door and disappears into the house. My sister looks as confused as I feel, probably also wondering why Mami keeps running off lately. Papi takes over at the grill.

"Is she still mad because of Ju's homework?" Lah asks him.

"No."

But I can't shake the sense that the reason my mother's upset again does have to do with my project. How can a measly school assignment cause so much drama, for so long?

"Why don't you girls set the table?" my father says, way too cheerfully, like he's trying to distract us.

It works on my sister. Her face lights up. "Oh! We're eating outside?" He nods. She jumps off a chair onto the deck. "Yay-ay-ay."

I sigh and turn to him. "Should I set it for three or four?"

"Four," he says, tsking as if I should know better. "She'll come back when she's ready."

79

I open the sliding door and Lah bounds into the house. I follow her inside. Through the glass, my father is still visible, standing by the grill and shaking his head.

I tug at my necklace.

"Are you mad too?" Lah asks.

"No." I grab the paper plates and cups, then hand her the napkins and plastic utensils. She sets the doll up on the table so she can grab hold of the caddy with two hands, grunting like it weighs a ton.

Back outside, Papi continues with the fake happy voice. "Heavy stuff you got there, kiddo?" He ruffles Lah's hair. She nods. He flashes a big grin and takes the caddy. She lets her shoulders fall forward as if he's taken a tower of bricks from her hands.

I wish he could relieve me of the weight in the pit of my stomach that easily. But some heavy truth is hiding behind that deep, happy voice. He must know why our mother's acting so strange. It's weighing him down, too.

I grab the mystery envelope from the drawer in the nightstand, then collapse onto my bed. It's finally time to see what the private investigator mailed to my mother so many years ago. I shake out the contents onto my navy blue quilt. It's a greeting card with a big cartoon duck wearing overalls and holding hands with a duckling in a pink dress. Across the top is printed: Hope Your Birthday Is Ducky!

A kid's birthday card. What the heck? I frown and open it to read the inside.

Dear Little Justina,

Happy 1st birthday!

Love,

Wilson and Renee

So this W. D. Martin is not a woman, but a man. A guy named Wilson. But...who the heck is Renee?

My mind races, trying to think of uncles, aunts, or family friends named Wilson and Renee. Shouldn't there have been some other mention of these people who were that close to me as a baby? I mean, they used the word 'love' to sign the card. Surely I would've heard stories about them. Unless...unless my parents don't want me to know who they are. Or else why stash this card away in the back compartment of an old trunk, along with a stack of recipes? Strong evidence they're keeping Wilson and Renee's identities hidden from me. But why?

I check the envelope again, hoping to find some other clue.

And I do. A small faded photo's stuck to the inside. A note is attached with a rusty paperclip. In the same scratchy handwriting that's on the envelope and inside the card, these words are scrawled: **Renee snapped** *this shot. **Thought it might be a nice one for you to give Justina...when she's old enough to understand.** -WDM*

Old enough to understand what? I slip the paper off the picture. There I am, just a baby, sitting on the floor with some man I don't ever remember seeing before in my life. It looks like we were having a blast, both of us clapping. I reach back to any scrap of memory with this man. Nothing there. Until I hold the blurry snapshot inches away and gasp, not believing my eyes. But it's there, clear as anything.

The man has amber eyes, like me.

Mami's voice echoes in my mind—*Puerto Ricans come in all shades.* My stomach flip-flops. Sure, it's true. But what if that's not the case for *me?* What if there's some completely different explanation for my blond hair and amber eyes, and it has to do with this Wilson and Renee? Could I have been...adopted?

No, that can't be it. The whole idea seems too crazy to even contemplate. Chances are, this card and photo probably mean nothing. I've just read too many detective stories and now I'm creating a mystery where there isn't one. I won't even bother writing these...these non-clues in my casebook.

I glance at my cell phone on the nightstand and consider calling Ig to get his opinion. But I wouldn't be able to handle it if he was mean to me right now. Or just hung up.

In the window, my blurred reflection resembles a watercolor portrait. Vague and undefined. Not Ju, but someone else. Maybe this whole time, I've been a master of disguise without even knowing it.

So instead of calling Ig, I dial Sara's number. Because it's a cold hard fact that she's the perfect one to help me with what needs to be done right now. I'm ready to change myself. To uncover the real me.

When Sara picks up, I blurt out, "Is your sister home?"

THROWBACK: FIFTH GRADE
HOW TO BOX YOURSELF IN

Back in fifth grade we were all sent home with a survey. Questions about study habits, extracurricular activities, number of household members. Easy stuff. At least until I turned to the last page, which read:

Please indicate your ethnic and racial background.

Ethnic background:
☐ **Hispanic or Latino (of any race)**

Racial background:
☐ **White**
☐ **Black/African American**
☐ **American Indian/Alaska Native**
☐ **Asian/Pacific Islander**

I wrote an X in the Hispanic or Latino box right away. Then sat back, tugging at my coquí *charm, staring at the racial background categories.*

"Which is the right box to check?" I'd asked my parents. "How do I know?"

"There isn't one right box, m'ija," Mami said. "Most Latinos are a mix of Native, African, and European heritage. Sometimes Asian, too."

"So do I check them all off?"

"Well." Papi tilted his head from one side to the other. "This survey's more about how you identify yourself."

"You mean, like, when I'm at school?"

My parents exchanged confused glances. "Don't you see yourself the same way all the time?"

I shrugged. "I guess."

Truth was, until then, I'd never really considered which racial group I belonged to. But it seemed suddenly it was time to decide.

I'd sat there and stared at the survey, baffled. Thinking how much simpler life had been back in second grade, when I could just point to a globe and say, "I was born here. But my parents were born there."

CHAPTER TWELVE:
MASTER OF DISGUISE

When Papi turns onto Sara Baker's street, he clears his throat and says, "What happened at lunch today wasn't your fault, Justina."

I turn away to stare out the window, not bothering to answer. What can I say: *Tell me about Wilson and Renee?*

But those words are impossible to spit out no matter how badly I want to know the truth. I can't act like everything's okay, either. Tears threaten to spill over but I force them back, focusing on my plan. If my parents are going to keep my real past a secret, I'll just have to create my own identity.

And that's exactly why I've asked to be dropped off at Sara's place.

"Thanks," I mutter before slamming the car door.

I haven't been to Sara's house in a long time. When we started middle school, she decided she was too cool to hang out with me anymore. And now, here I am about to get a makeover. I can't believe it's come to this.

Through the front screen door, I peer into the foyer. There's the towering Grandfather clock made of reddish-brown wood that I once stubbed my toe on. That was years ago at one of Sara's huge birthday parties. Well, we won't be playing hide and seek today, that's for sure.

I ring the bell.

A voice calls from the back of the house, "Door's open!"

I let myself in and stroll toward the kitchen. Mr. Baker is seated at the table surrounded by stacks of paper. He's an English teacher at the high school. "Why hello, Justina! It's been so long. How's the family?"

Ha! If he only knew. "Fine."

"Good to hear." He pats a stack of essays. "Don't mind the mess. I'm grading papers. Sara's in the basement."

"Thanks. Nice seeing you." I smile at him to be polite, then skip down the steps. Sara's lounging on a leather sofa in front of a huge flat-screen, playing a video game where giant snakes fight and spit at each other. "I'm so going to poison you!" she screams.

Her older sister, Megan, tosses long frosted blond hair over one shoulder and narrows her eyes at me, assessing the damage. "Sara says you had a dye disaster." She grips a fistful of my hair. "Hmm. This'll be great practice. My instructor says I need more experience with problem hair."

I wonder now if I've made a mistake coming here. I feel like a lab rat with frizzy fur.

"Ah man!" Sara tosses down the control pad and perks up. "Don't worry. Megan's the best with a flatiron." She flops back against the sofa and starts a new game.

I sit in front of a small table prepped just like a hair salon's, only Megan uses an adjustable office chair in front of a large mirror mounted on the wall.

She taps my *coquí* charm. "Cool necklace. That's one of those Mexican frogs, right?"

"Puerto Rican. It was my grandmother's." Or was it? I push away recollections of my attic search and focus instead on my transformation. "Can you flip up the ends a little?"

"Sure thing." She uses a spray bottle to soak my hair, then piles most of it on top of my head with a huge clip. She reaches for the hairdryer and a gigantic round brush.

"Wait! Can you dye it back to blond first?"

She smiles at me in the mirror. "Of course." She rummages through a crate and fishes out a box of dye. "Here. Sandy Beach all right?"

"Sounds good." Any shade at all will do. As long as it isn't Feliciano Brown.

***

Two hours later Megan drops Sara and me off at the mall. I smooth my stick-straight blond-again hair as we enter through the food court, then tug at the sleeves of the light pink hoodie I'm wearing. Sara's hoodie. Back at the house, she said the only way she'd be seen in public with me is if I borrowed some of her clothes. For a moment, I feel bad that the beaded tunic Titi Nessa made me is stuffed into the messenger bag, which Sara also forced me to leave in Megan's jeep.

Sara hooks her arm in mine as we pass the glass elevator looming over a two-story fountain, and gushes, "Wow, this is a way better look for you!"

We roam the packed mall as if we've been friends forever. As if she isn't just taking pity on me because I'm trying to catch the person who's determined to ruin her big opening night.

"So Monday, you'll be back on the case, right? 'Cause it's such a distraction not knowing who's the maniac trying to derail my performance."

"Yeah." I stick my hands in the pockets of the hoodie, which are already stuffed with my phone and wallet. "I'll question Raj first thing. He's been staying late to help build the set, you know. Need to find out what he's doing during the fifteen minutes between rehearsal and crew call."

"What?" She spins to face me. "It's not him."

"How would you know?"

I wasn't expecting to also have to be Nancy Drew during this shopping trip, but it's a revelation too good to ignore.

"Okay. Now, you can't tell anyone." She lowers her eyes.

"What?" I whisper. "That he likes you?"

Sara blushes. "How'd you know?"

Instead of ratting out Gunther, I shrug and peer at a storefront window that sells nothing but baseball caps. "Oh, you know. Word gets around."

"Well, here's the thing. Me and Raj...we're not *together* together, but kinda together." She giggles and shuffles her feet. "We, like, hang backstage by ourselves for a few minutes until we hear Mr. Vincent start crew call. Raj brings me candy. Swedish Fish. Chocolate. M&Ms and stuff. It's sweet." She sighs.

I fight off the urge to gag. "Uh huh. So why's it a big secret?"

"Please. The way my friends gossip?"

"Thought you weren't supposed to eat near the stage?"

"Another reason you can't tell a soul. I only say all this to clear his name." She leans into me. "My point is, he wouldn't have *time* to destroy the set between rehearsal and crew. I'm his alibi."

"You and the Swedish Fish." I snort.

Sara giggles. "You're so funny, Ju!"

And just like that, I'm giggling too. We find the As-Seen-On-TV vendor cart where Megan said I'd get the best deal on a flatiron. Three other girls who look like they're in high school are reluctantly watching a buff sales guy straighten long black hair on a mannequin head. When he turns to us, they scurry off.

I point to several flatirons hanging on the side of the cart. "How much are those?"

"Hold on." He turns over a price list in a plastic sleeve and shows it to me. The standard model costs more than what I've saved since my last birthday.

I hand the list back. "Thanks."

"How long does it take to blow out your hair?" the guy asks.

Who knows? I tell him forty minutes, because that's how long it took Megan to do it.

He takes down the pro-deluxe model. "With this product it'll take half of the time. My girlfriend swears by it."

"Great." I smile at him. "Can't afford it."

He hangs the iron back on its display hook, then rummages through a drawer under the cash register and pulls out a mini-iron. "Hey, it's your lucky day. There's one travel-size left."

Still feels like too much at thirty dollars, but at least I have enough to buy it. After paying, I find Sara at the next vendor cart, bent at the waist, trying to write upside-down with an astronaut pen.

"So," I say. "Where do we go for the cool clothes?"

She pops right-side-up again, making her ponytail whip around dramatically. "I know just the place," she says, then yanks my arm and hauls me along as if I'm a little red wagon.

I kind of feel like the kid, and she's the parent here. But I'm fine with her being in control. Because here's another cold hard fact: I'd never find my way around this huge, crowded mall without her.

CHAPTER THIRTEEN:
CHANGING

Slow saxophone music pours like melted butter through ceiling speakers in the dressing room of the designer discount store. A sign on the door says, NO MORE THAN 6 ITEMS. But the lady who hands out the little plastic number tags has disappeared. So at least thirty outfits are hanging in this tiny dressing room with me. Sara keeps coming back with armfuls of clothes. It's apparently her idea of fun. So far, I've found a couple pairs of jeans, sweatpants with a matching hoodie and three cool tops. But nothing I put on makes me feel like a different person.

"Got a bunch of colors of skinny jeans. Plus a sweater dress." She flings the new load over the top of the stall door. Suddenly it's raining clothes. "Come out and show me what works."

After organizing the newest batch onto the overflowing hooks, I hold the soft, knitted dress up against me. It's turquoise with three-quarter length sleeves. The hem stops a few inches above my knees. Girls come to school in much shorter dresses every day. But for *me* to wear this, would be—well, different.

Which is exactly what I need, right?

"Okay," I whisper to my reflection. "Let's do this."

I slide the dress over my head and smooth it out. Yes. Good. I'm almost there, but something's still holding me back. I unclasp the *coquí* necklace and hide it in one hand. Yep. That's it.

I open the dressing room door to get Sara's opinion.

She jumps up and down, clapping like I'm her very own life-sized Barbie. "Ooh! A new and improved Ju."

"Tina." I say. "That name fits me better now."

She smiles. "Perfect."

Of course, I know it'll be hard to get my parents to call me that. I know for sure Ig won't. But it's not like he's calling me by any name at all these days, so...

I rise on tiptoes to see what the dress will look like if I wore it with Mami's heels. "You think people at school will actually start calling me Tina?"

"Sure they will." Sara nods. "But if anyone forgets, I'll just totally remind them."

I shrug. "Gunther will probably still call me Feliciano."

Sara's eyes narrow. "Gunther Corrie?"

"In class, I mean."

"So you like him?" she asks way too loudly.

"Shh. No!" I close the door on her sly, goofy grin.

"He's invited to my par-ty on Sat-ur-day," she sings through the door, in a high yoo-hoo voice. "You should definitely come. In that dress."

She chatters on long enough for me to change back into the outfit borrowed from her. When I open the door again, she hands me a bunch of hangers. "You are coming, right?"

"Maybe." I let the door swing shut again.

It's almost dark when Megan drops me off at home. I climb the steps of our screened front porch, where Lah's perched on the swing with Delilah Juniorette in her lap and dozens of stuffed animals surrounding her. I try to slip by unnoticed. Mission Impossible.

She gawks, wide-eyed. "Why isn't your hair poufy anymore?"

Mami's suddenly in the doorway. "I was wondering if you'd be home in time for dinner." She stares at my hair, then down at the shopping bags. "Did you go to the mall?"

I squeeze past, dropping the new stuff near the steps. "Yeah. Needed some clothes. Used my birthday money."

"Titi Nessa left two new sweaters you asked her to make." She folds a kitchen towel in her hands, over and over, until it's a useless fat rectangle. "They're in your room."

"Oh. I forgot about those." I reach into one bag and fish out a box of brown hair dye. The last thing I bought at the mall. "Here you go."

"Thank you." She nods. "I could use a hand finishing dinner." She shuffles into the kitchen and I follow, even though I really want to take the shopping bags upstairs to my room. I start rinsing a pile of dirty dishes in the sink and loading them in the dishwasher.

Mami's quiet for a few minutes, but she turns her head a couple of times to glance at me. Like she's figuring out what it means that I went shopping without her for the first time. She puts the lid on a pot of rice that smells so delicious my stomach growls.

"Who did your hair?"

"Sara Baker's sister."

"Oh." She clears her throat. "Looks nice."

"Thanks." I grab a couple of mugs and fit them into the dishwasher.

"Giving up on brown hair?" She stares down at a serving spoon as if she's having a conversation with it, instead of me.

"Brown didn't really...fit." I reach for the spoon, but she doesn't let go.

"This is for the rice." She frowns. "Where's your necklace?"

"In my pocket." Now *I'm* talking to the spoon. "Why? Do you want it back?"

"No." When she lifts a juice glass, her hand starts to shake, like it did when she was grilling chicken at lunch. Now it feels like that argument happened months ago. I take the glass so she won't drop it. "I'll finish rinsing."

She's quiet again. Then finally asks if I'm still watching a movie with my father later tonight. I'd completely forgotten we planned to finish *The Hound of the Baskervilles.* "I guess. If Papi remembers." Sweat prickles my scalp, threatening to frizz the roots of my hair. I shove my hand in my pocket and clutch my *coquí* charm. Maybe I should tell him never mind. But with all this craziness in the air, it sure would be great to get lost in an old movie. Anything to forget the uncertainty of here and now.

Papi gets the DVD player ready while I lounge on the sofa with a bowl of tortilla chips on my lap. He glances up at me and smiles. "I'll try not to fall asleep this time, eh?"

"Okay," I mumble, stuffing more crunchy chips into my mouth.

Lah runs in wearing cow-patterned footie pajamas. She squeezes in between me and Papi, then peeks up at him, raising her eyebrows. "Tea Time?"

I place the snack bowl on the side table so she won't knock it over. "We're watching a movie."

"We can play and watch at the same time," she insists.

"No one invited you." I stretch my legs up onto the sofa, hoping she'll get the hint that it's too crowded with her there.

Instead, she crawls onto Papi's lap. "But I can stay, right?"

"She'll have nightmares," I say, expecting him to agree. But he's busy fiddling with the flatscreen remote, adjusting the volume.

"I'll close my eyes if it gets scary." Lah plants footie-covered feet against my legs and pushes.

"*Claro*, you can stay, Delilah. Remember, Justina? You were your sister's age the first time you saw this film." He gives me a look that says, *Please. Don't start.*

"You'll pay attention to her instead of the movie." Or me.

Lah kicks me again while making it seem like she's only snuggling up to Papi.

"Quit it, Lah!" I jump up and turn to him. "This is our first movie night in forever and she's ruining it."

"She just wants to sit here with us," he says.

Lah wiggles back until his arm is around her. They look like one of those sample photos that come inside a new picture frame: *Fathers and Daughters Are Special.*

"She wants to be near you. Not me." Maybe he doesn't want to be near me, either. "Know what? Forget it. I'll let you spend time with your favorite daughter."

His eyes widen. "Justina!"

Your real daughter.

I turn to leave and knock over the snack bowl. A hail of chips flies out to litter the carpet. My feet crunch across a bunch of them. "You didn't even notice my hair."

He straightens in his seat as much as he can with my sister leaning on him. "Of course I noticed."

"Then why didn't you say anything?"

Lah sits up. "I did."

"It's very pretty," he says.

I fold my arms and try to keep my voice from quivering. "You're just saying that now."

"Hey." It's his no-nonsense voice. "Look at me, please."

I do as he says, pretending my face is made of stone.

"Your hair's nice this way, but I still love your curls," he says gently. "They suit you. You're my daughter with the curls."

No. With or without curls, I'm not—

"I always think you're beautiful," he adds. *"Siempre."*

"I'm not—" *Your daughter.*

Forget the stone face. Tears wet my cheeks. My stupid nose is running. My head pounding like a stage-set hammer.

Papi slides Lah off and stands. He takes my chin in one hand. "Yes, you are beautiful. No matter what you do to your hair. No matter if it's curly or straight. Blond or brown." He smiles. "Even shaved bald."

He doesn't understand. This isn't about being beautiful. "Not like it matters! I'll never look like I belong in this family."

Both of them stare at me with wide, matching brown eyes. Clueless.

I run out of the room. In the hallway, on the hardwood floor, I slip on some greasy broken chips stuck to the bottom of my socks. I reach out hoping to catch the wall to keep from tripping and, instead, end up skidding smack into the door to Papi's office, falling to the floor inside. I land in the dark on hands and knees, trying to catch my breath. No use, I'm full-out bawling now. But my loud sobs don't drown out a crash as something falls onto the desk above my head.

I use the office chair to drag myself upright. Click on the small lamp, which shines on the deformed Maltese Falcon. That's what fell. Now it's broken in two. I take both pieces of the ugly thing and shove it into the back of a desk drawer, behind a bunch of files. Then wipe my face with one sleeve and turn off the lamp.

I race from the office and up the stairs into my room. It's the only safe place for me now. The shopping bags from earlier still sit on the bed. I pull all the new clothes out and lay them flat. Outfits that belong to a cool new girl named Tina. I stuff two pillowcases with all the

Craft-e-Shop clothing from my drawers and closet. In the end there's not enough room, so I fill some duffel bags, too.

All of Ju's old clothes go deep into a back corner of the closet. Three out of four dresser drawers are still empty. But I don't care.

I dig out the *coquí* necklace that's been in my pocket this whole time. Look down at it lying in my palm for only a moment, and then shove it into the nightstand. I don't need it anymore.

I cut the tags off all my new clothes and put them away. This is my wardrobe now. Clothes for the real me. Maybe I can't do anything about belonging in this family, in this house. Or about how I feel on the inside. But I can change some things on the outside. Like fitting into Sara's crowd at school.

CHAPTER FOURTEEN:
RESEARCH BLUES

After the final bell on Monday, I head straight to the school library to research the mysterious Wilson Martin. The computer lab is empty. I slide into the closest station, happy to be off my feet. Before this weekend, I'd have never even dreamed of wearing my mother's black heels. But according to Sara, I just had to wear them with my new skinny jeans and crimson blouse.

The screen prompts me to input my user name and password. And here's the thing about changing who you are—in the last place you'd expect, there are always reminders of exactly who you were trying not to be. I type in: *mystrygrl*. Hit the tab key, then hammer out: *JulgBFF*. I fish out the envelope I'd stuffed into the black bucket handbag grabbed from my mother's closet this morning. Then type Wilson Martin's return address in the search box.

The previous search led me to Ms. W. D. Martin, Private Detective. Talk about a false lead. If I've learned anything from mystery books and detective movies, it's that you never solve a case on the first try. You just have to keep going after the cold hard facts.

I scan the list of files that comes up and click on an archived announcement in a small town newspaper from ten years ago. It's for the grand opening of 'Connecticut's Premier Lawn and Garden Center.' It seems they've knocked down the condos where Wilson Martin once lived. It's now a state-of-the-art gardening store.

Another search: Renee Martin. Thousands of hits. I click on the first few results that take me to pages for a bunch of different women. A French-Canadian speed-skating champion. An African-American puppeteer turned head of a university art program. An eighty-year-old food blogger from Kansas. None of the women seem like they could be the right Renee Martin. But then I don't really have much to go on. A blind search is useless.

I groan and mutter, "The mystery continues."

After logging out, I slide the envelope back into the purse, and head to our club's secret meeting spot, squeezing past a cart near the end of the biography aisle.

Gunther is perched on the footstool watching a video of basketball dunks on his Smartphone.

"Hey," I say.

He glances up. "Oh. Hey. Your hair."

"Sara's sister did it." I tuck it behind my ears and smile.

"Looks nice, Feliciano." Gunther smiles back, all crooked and cute.

I take out Mami's compact and check. "I told Sara you'd still call me that."

He slips the phone into his backpack. "Heard about the name change."

Yes, Sara's been busy spreading the word. All day people have been calling me Tina. "Actually, it's more like an everything change."

He raises his eyebrows. "Whoa. Sounds major."

I dump Mami's purse and my books onto the floor and relax on a footstool a few feet from him. "Yeah. That's the point."

"Does this mean no more detective work?"

Now that I think about it, mysteries really are Ju's thing. Her old thing with Papi. Her thing with Ig. But it's not like I can back out of helping Sara. At least, not yet. "I'll stick with it until we solve this case."

"Oh, good. Because I really want to catch this guy," Gunther says, then adds quickly, "Or girl."

"Here's the latest." I open the casebook. "Already crossed off Janine and Raj. Changed their statuses in the notes too."

SERIOUSLAND

<u>CAST LIST:</u>
~~Lady Luciana—Sara Baker~~
Sir Serious—Franklin Diaz
The Jester—Ayesha Malloy
~~The Servant—Janine Petite~~
~~The Beggar—Elizabeth Moore~~
~~The Prince—Raj Gupta~~
~~Female Understudy—Nina Minchi~~
~~Male Understudy—Seth Bernstein~~

Set Construction/Tech Crew:
~~Seth Bernstein, Gunther Corrie, Nina Minchi, Elijah Roberts~~

And I write:

RAJ: ~~*Person of interest/current lead suspect*~~, has alibi
- Plays "The Prince"
- Unofficially on set crew
- Has crush on Sara
- Sara is his alibi

105

JANINE: Not a current suspect

- Plays "The Servant"

- Doesn't know how to spell

Gunther hands the notebook back. "What does spelling have to do with anything?"

"Yesterday, our sub in English had us sign a piece of paper to record attendance. Sara wasn't there yet. Janine signed Sara's name so she wouldn't be marked late. But she spelled it with an H." I slap the casebook shut.

"Oh." Gunther's eyes grow wide. "And the vandal *knows* Sara spells her name without the H because that's how it was on the scenery."

"Exactly."

He smirks. "Elementary, my dear Feliciano."

There's a creaking nearby. I gaze at the aisle of biographies, but it's empty. "I haven't had a chance to interview Franklin Diaz or Ayesha Malloy yet."

"They should both be at Sara's party," he says. "You're going, right?"

Another creak. Gunther leans over me and peeks around the corner. So close I smell his citrus shampoo. A cart in the aisle tips over and books go flying everywhere. A fat hardcover edition of Dolly Madison's biography lands inches from my foot. Wow, that would've hurt.

"Ow," moans a familiar voice. Behind the fallen cart, the cuff of Ig's white long-sleeve shirt is caught under one wheel.

I come around to stand over him. "You okay?"

"Um." He grimaces as if something else broke along with his dignity. "Trying to find out why...you changed your name."

Gunther snorts. "Couldn't just ask, Soto?"

"Of course not." I toss my silky-smooth hair over one shoulder. "He doesn't talk to me anymore."

"Oh yeah?" Ig pushes his wavy mop out of his eyes with a free hand. "What am I doing now?"

"Hmm." I pick up the Dolly Madison biography. "Researching famous first ladies?"

Gunther slings his backpack over one shoulder. "See you tomorrow, guys." He rolls his eyes at me and then runs off down the aisle.

I turn back to Ig. "Seriously, you okay?"

He closes his eyes. "Can you help with my sleeve?"

I loosen the trapped cloth. Ig turns the cart right side up. I kneel and help him set the books back on the shelf even though I'm still pretty mad at him for spying.

"Ju...I mean, Ti—sorry, but I can't call you that name." He rubs at the greasy track the wheel left on his sleeve. "So, you and Gunther, huh?"

"*What?* Why in the world would you think that?"

"Are you going to that party?" he asks in a cold, hard voice.

I can't believe him. "Are you jealous of *Gunther?*"

107

"No," Ig says immediately. "I don't see you like that, okay?"

"Well, Gunther doesn't either." I cross my arms. "We're just friends."

"New name, new hair, new clothes, new friends." Smirking, Ig rattles off this list like it's all a big joke.

"You're the one who stopped talking to me!"

"I was stressed out, Ju." The veins in his forehead are bulging. "You knew that, but you were more concerned about Sara's stupid problem than mine." He looks away, swallowing, as if he's about to cry.

"That's not true." It's not like he's the only other person in the world with a stupid problem! I wish I could tell him everything. Like, I really do understand how he feels about the genetics project because it's ruining my life, too. "I thought investigating her mystery would make you feel better. Honest."

Ig looks up, right at me. "You didn't need to completely change. I mean, what are you trying to prove?"

Prove? I don't know what to say to that. My hand falls to my neck, going for the *coquí* charm. But of course, it's gone. Which is totally fine.

I don't need it.

I let my hair fall forward to conceal the tears gathering in the corners of my eyes. "I'm not trying to prove anything. Gotta go."

Then I grab up all my things, jaw clenched, and race away through the biography aisle.

Because if I stayed Ig might keep reminding me of how great things had seemed, back when life was all about simple things. Like old mystery stories and a good game of dominoes.

THROWBACK: SIXTH GRADE
DON'T KNOW WHY

One day last year I was over at Ig's house playing dominoes like we always did. Ig's mother had whistled as she set one of his planet coffee mugs filled with steaming café con leche *in front of each of us. Just then I laid the double-six domino out on the kitchen table.*

"Take it easy on him, eh?" She winked. "Maybe even let him win a round or two."

I took a sip of the hot, sweet, creamy coffee, waiting for him to take his turn.

"Where's mine?" Javier, Ig's older brother, asked as he sauntered into the kitchen.

"How about a por favor *or* gracias*?" But Mrs. Soto handed him a Mars mug anyway.*

"Please, Ma. Thank you, Ma." Javier took a sip and closed his eyes in ecstasy. "Mmm."

I'd stirred my coffee with a spoon, making the light brown liquid into a whirlpool while Ig still studied his domino tiles.

"Let me guess, you're kicking his butt again, Ju." Javier had snorted. "I swear, I don't get how you're so good at dominoes when you're white as Casper."

"What do you mean?" I narrowed my eyes at him.

110

*"You know...that friendly, fat little ghost?" He smirked.
"Got the whole* blancita *thing going on. You probably got
ancestors from northern Spain who thought they were
better than everyone else. "*

My mouth fell open but no words came out.

Ig frowned. "What the heck, Javi?"

*Ms. Soto had said then, in a dangerously quiet, even
tone, "Why would you say something like that to Justina?"*

*"Don't know." He shrugged. "My friends always joke
around like that."*

*Ig played the six blank tile. "Sounds like your friends
are all jerks."*

*I stood up from my chair and glared at his brother. "I
don't know if my ancestors thought they were better than
anyone else, but I don't think that. What does that have to
do with dominoes, anyway?"*

*Then I'd run out of the room, holding back tears.
Collapsing onto a brown sofa in the small family room, I
had stared at Ms. Soto's nursing school textbooks piled on
the side table, wondering if I was overreacting.*

*After a couple minutes, Javier came up and cleared his
throat in the doorway. "I'm sorry, Ju." His gaze was fixed
on the floral-print carpet. "Pretty stupid stuff to say.
When my friends make jokes like that, everyone laughs
like it's comedy hour. I guess for us it's no big deal to..."*

"To call people names?"

*"Yeah, well..." He looked away and sipped his coffee.
"Anyhow, it wasn't cool. I understand if you're mad."*

I took a deep breath and asked, "So. When will it become no big deal?"

His eyes met mine, looking startled. "What?"

"The way I'm supposed to look. Supposed to be. Checking off boxes on surveys—"

"Whoa. Hold up." He sat next to me on the sofa. "You have to fill those out too? I swear, at college, it's like every week I have to fill out something that asks for my race and ethnicity. And I always think, if they're gonna ask a really complicated question like that, they should at least give the option to answer in essay format."

"Right?" I laughed. "Then we could explain about things like playing dominoes...or how coquís are the most important frog on the face of the earth."

"The way Mami starts a sentence in Spanish but ends it in English."

I clapped my hands. "Putting hay under the bed for Three Kings Day!"

"¡Café con leche!" He hoisted his mug in triumph.

I shrugged. "Can't fit all that into those little boxes."

"Nah." Javier looked at me sideways. "Sure can't."

We sat there in silence for a moment. Then he turned to me again, totally serious. "Aren't you supposed to be kicking my little bro's butt in dominoes right now?"

I smiled and stood up. Before I left the room I looked down at Javier. "Ever just wanna be who you are without all the check-marks?"

He nodded. "Sometimes."

"Me too." *And then I'd turned, heading into the kitchen, back to the sweet familiar smell of* café con leche.

CHAPTER FIFTEEN:
BREAKING THE RULES

I consider skipping breakfast this morning but am finally lured downstairs to the kitchen by the smell of bacon, hash browns, and coffee.

When I land on the bottom step, I hear my mother's voice whispering, "My sister says she sees it all the time with her students. Claims they're searching hard for a place to fit in. But I told her Justina's just going through a phase."

"Nessa has a point," Papi says. "Justina's changed her hair color twice now. Changed all her clothes. Even her name. All since the assignment. *Corazón*, I think it's time."

"Time for what?" I come into the kitchen then. "Morning."

Papi smiles. "Hey, Sleeping Beauty."

Mami slides off the plastic cover she was using to keep my plate warm and pours me a tall glass of orange juice. "What took you so long?"

"Tired, I guess." I slide into the chair across from Lah and, suddenly ravenous, shove an entire slice of salty bacon into my mouth.

"We were just talking about you." Papi eyes Mami across the table. "Weren't we, Alana?"

She clears her throat. "Yes. Saying how happy you'd be when you found out I got four tickets to Buster's Big Top Spectacular at the county college tonight."

Lah squeals. "I'm telling Delilah Juniorette we're going to the circus!" She runs upstairs, dropping her napkin halfway across the kitchen.

Papi sighs and shakes his head. Obviously, the circus wasn't what he wanted Mami to talk about.

"Well?" She picks up Lah's napkin from the tiles. "Aren't you excited?"

I shrug and wash down the bacon with some orange juice. "Thanks. But I have plans tonight."

"I've bought four tickets and we're using all of them," my mother insists.

"You can't force me to go." I stick my fork in a fried slice of potato. "Anyhow, the circus is for little kids. I used to like it, but not anymore."

"You're coming with us, and that's final," Papi says.

"Why? So we can argue about my project again? Or maybe you can explain to me all about how I'm going through a *phase*."

Mami raises her eyebrows. "You were eavesdropping?"

Papi holds up one hand. "Now, Alana—"

"I just happened to hear you on my way down the steps," I say.

My mother crosses her arms. "Finish your food. It's getting cold."

"I'm not hungry." I stand and pick up my plate. "It's no big deal that I've changed some stuff, okay? Just realized...I wasn't a good fit. That's all."

"A good fit where?" my father asks, frowning.

"Anywhere."

I put the plate in the sink and run upstairs before I can see their reactions. Slamming the door to my bedroom, I lean against it, panting like I've just run a mile. Their voices are muffled but still sound angry coming up through the floor. On the other side of the wall, Lah's crying in her room. She must've heard all the yelling. Part of me wants to tell her I'm only trying to avoid a disaster at the circus. To make sure she has a good time tonight. But I stay in my room and jerk the pillow over my head to block out all the shouting I've caused.

This absolutely proves one hard cold fact. Whenever I'm not around, it's better for everyone.

It's afternoon when I wake up again. The house is quiet. I grab my phone from the nightstand and send Sara a text*: coming to ur party, sleeping over.*

She texts back: ***my sis will pick u up in 2 hrs @ end of ur blck***

I shower and use the flatiron on my hair until it's smooth as the satin pajamas my mother wears sometimes. I've gotten to know her wardrobe better lately from all the borrowing of shoes and handbags. For Sara's party, it's tall black boots and a long dark-gray jacket to throw over my turquoise dress, since it's cold outside. I grab the black purse I borrowed the other day and a packed overnight bag. Then I write a note to my parents and leave it propped on the kitchen table on my way out.

Sleeping over at Sara's. Have fun at the circus. Lah can invite Chloe in my place. - Tina

It's already dark outside. I walk a block to meet Megan's car at the corner of my street.

"Hey. Pretty good straightening job," she says, eyeing my hair as I climb into the passenger seat. It's nice and warm inside the Jeep with heat flowing from the vents.

I've absolutely made the right choice. And tonight will definitely be a better night for everyone because of it.

CHAPTER SIXTEEN:
SARA'S PARTY

Sara's house is filled with a spicy autumn scent. Megan blows out a rust-colored candle on the hall table. "Whoops. Dad would kill me if he knew I left this burning. Good thing he's teaching a class tonight." She takes off her windbreaker and tosses it on a heap of outerwear piled on a tan leather sofa in the family room.

"In case of emergency, I'm upstairs," she says, then bolts up to the second floor.

I dump the overnight bag, purse, and jacket on top of everyone else's stuff and head for the basement. Downstairs about ten people are watching Gunther and Sara play that snake video game on the large flat-screen. In another corner, three guys cheer on a girl doing back flips. Past Megan's salon area Janine Petit and Ayesha Malloy fling their arms back and forth, shooting a puck across an air hockey table.

"Hey, Tina!" Janine shouts.

It takes a second to realize she means me. "Oh...hi."

"Why'd you pause the game?" I hear Gunther shout.

Sara elbows him. "Would you hold on a sec? Tina's here."

There's that crooked smile again as he spots me. "Oh. Cool dress."

"Thanks." I join the crowd by the television. "So who's winning?"

"The cheater," Sara says, knocking her shoulder into Gunther's.

"Hey, who's that girl?" I hear someone ask from across the room.

Another voice answers, "Oh, her? That's *Tina.*"

Gunther and I chomp on yummy two-bite brownies while lounging on beanbag chairs. It's weird having a conversation with him in front of people, instead of hidden in a dark corner of the school library.

He leans into me and whispers, "We can rule out Diaz as a suspect."

"Did you talk to him?"

"Yeah. Now don't stare, but take a look at him over there." He tilts his head toward the far corner of the basement, near the hot-water heater.

I sneak a peek at Franklin Diaz. He's obviously running through choreography and singing to himself. "He's rehearsing *now?*"

Gunther raises his eyebrows. "He said admissions reps from the local arts magnet high school are coming to see the eighth graders perform. It's part of the application process. He's freaking that he'll run out of time to really nail his performance. According to him, the entire future will be decided by how well this show goes."

I see Gunther's point: clearly, the last thing Franklin would want is for another actor to screw up and make the play look stupid. "Sounds like they found the perfect person to play Sir Serious," I say.

Gunther laughs and I join in. Still, it can't compare to the giggle fests I've had with Ig.

No, no, no. Stop thinking about Ig!

I clear my throat. "So I've made up my mind. Once I'm done with Sara's case, I'm taking a break from mysteries."

"Huh." He squints like he's trying hard to figure me out. "Maybe you're the mystery now."

"Oh please." But he's got a point. I've been so busy trying to nail down Tina's appearance, I haven't thought about who this new version of me really is. Ju was a good student. A responsible older sister. Papi's little girl. Ig's best friend. But Tina? I don't know who in the world she is yet.

"Didn't mean to bum you out." Gunther sinks his head back on the beanbag chair. "What's Soto's deal? You, like, hate each other now?"

I glance down at my plate, picking at the last brownie crumbs. "No, not at all."

Raj rushes past, tossing M&Ms over one shoulder, trying to fend off Sara and the crew. They're chasing him around the basement armed with bags of marshmallows.

Gunther brushes a few M&Ms from his lap. "Because it kind of seems like you don't need him anymore."

Only then does it finally dawn on me. Ig must think that too.

But of course I need him! I could never tell Gunther, Sara, or anyone else at this party about what's going on right now in my family. They'd never understand. What was I thinking? Poor Ig.

"I have to go." I jump up and start for the stairs.

Sara runs into me clutching a half-empty bag of marshmallows, shrieking, "Food fight!"

"Sorry, I've gotta leave."

"What?" She frowns. "But you were sleeping over."

"Not anymore, I—"

She lowers her voice. "But you can't. It was going so good with you and Gunther."

Still, from across the basement, he looks way more interested in the food fight than in talking to me. "There's somewhere important I need to be."

She gapes at me. "Important?"

"No! I don't mean...I had fun, Sara. Really." I give her a quick hug because she looks like I've hurt her feelings. "See you Monday, okay?"

Seth Bernstein runs past and snatches away her bag of marshmallows.

"Hey," she yells, turning away to chase after him. "That's totally stealing!" And just like that, she's over me leaving the party.

I dash up the steps, past the towering clock on my way into the living room. Grab my things and zip the jacket as high as it'll go. Then rush out the front door and down the porch steps, in such a big hurry it's a few moments before I realize it's raining. Really, really hard.

THROWBACK: FOURTH GRADE
WHAT HAPPENED TO MY HAIR

I guess there could be no worse bad hair day than the one in fourth grade when Papi dropped me off at Ig's house. I must've been a scary sight standing on the front stoop with my head a knotted mess. Eyes red and swollen because I'd spent the whole afternoon crying. I'd tried to style my own hair for Ig's piano recital, "I can do it myself," I'd told Mami. Even after two hours of fussing with the frizz. I was too proud to let her anywhere near my head, though my arms felt like they might fall off.

Ig's mother had gasped when she saw me. "Justina! ¿Que pasó to your hair?"

Ig shouted down from the end of the hallway. "Yeah, what happened?"

I swallowed back a sob. "I w-wanted to make it smoother but it wouldn't stay. Now it's tangled and even bigger than before!" I stomped my feet, crying, "Ugh, I HATE MY HAIR!"

"Go take your shower, Ignacio," Ms. Soto said.

She'd dragged a stool from the kitchen into the living room. "Here. Sit, mamita." *As stubborn as I'd been about doing things all by myself at home, I'd felt incredibly relieved when she asked, "Do you want one or two French braids?" Ms. Soto can style any type of hair into neat,*

124

perfect braids—it's her specialty. "Ay mira, *you've got such beautiful hair, Justina,"* she'd said *from behind me, already at work.* "Never say you hate it."

What did she know? She wore her neat brown hair short.

"But it m-makes me look weird. Different. Sticks up in every direction. I w-wish I had wavy hair like my sister's."
My eyes welled up. I winced as Ms. Soto twisted the hair tighter against my scalp.

"Oh, si." *She laughed softly.* "And in a few years she'll want hair just like yours."

Yeah right, *I'd thought then.* Who in the world would ever want to look like me?

CHAPTER SEVENTEEN:
IG'S PLACE

Twenty minutes later I'm standing out on the back stoop of Ig's place, borrowed jacket drenched. The bottom of my dress dripping. My hair's a mass of wet, heavy curls. The overnight bag, now soaked, might as well be filled with wet bricks.

The blinds over Ig's first-floor bedroom are shut, but the dim glow through them is a clue: He's using the book light I got for his birthday last year. I pick up a long fallen tree branch and do our special knock—one tap, three quick taps, two taps, two taps—like the opening rhythm of the Alfred Hitchcock show theme.

Shadows shift in the room. He cracks open the window.

"What're you doing here?" he whispers.

126

"I'll explain, but let me in. It's p-pouring."

"Sure. I'll be right out."

A couple minutes later he opens the back door, forehead creased with concern. "You're shivering."

I only nod as I step past. We're both silent trudging down the steps to the basement. It's shared by all three apartments in the house, but at this time of night, no one is around. The only sounds are the scratching of the soles of his slippers and the click of my boot heels against the linoleum.

Ig flicks on a light and disappears into the laundry room.

I've spent so much time in the main room of this basement. There's a mishmash of furniture that Ig's always told me "belongs to the basement," as if no one wants to claim the sagging sofa, color-clashing folding chairs, wobbly card table, and huge ancient television set. There are also three large sets of storage shelves, one for each apartment. The one belonging to Ig's family has remained pretty much the same since I've known him—stuffed with board games, tools, really old *Scientific American* magazines, and plastic bins of out-of-season clothes.

Ig comes back into the main room and hands me a pair of black sweatpants and a gray long-sleeve t-shirt that says RED HAWKS in thin block letters across the front. "Javier won't notice these missing."

"Th-thanks." I grit out through chattering teeth.

I go into the tiny basement bathroom, slip into the dry clothes, wring out my hair, and then creep back into the main room with my wet stuff wadded in a ball. A shiver seizes my shoulders as I step from the bathroom rug onto the cold cement basement floor.

"F-forgot to ask for s-socks."

Ig finds a white athletic pair in the laundry room. I yank them on quick while he hangs my limp wet dress over a folding chair. "Where'd you go in this thing?"

"Sara's party was t-tonight." I drop onto an old sofa, still freezing.

Ig turns on the space heater. "Let me guess. Gunther was there."

Not this again. "Gunther, Raj, Ayesha, Janine, Franklin. Lots of people. But after hanging there a couple hours, I just wanted to come see you. I really need to talk to someone who, you know, gets me. So I walked over here."

Ig frowns. "Wait a minute. Your parents don't know where you are?"

"They think I'm staying at Sara's. But believe me, they can use a night without me. And I can use a night without thinking about..."

I can't bring myself to say it. At least, not yet.

"What have you been up to? You ever get to the observatory to look through that telescope?"

He nods slowly, like he's trying to figure out my quick change of subject. At last he answers anyway. "My cousin Nilda went with me. Saw the moon, Neptune, the Andromeda galaxy. It was amazing."

I shrug. "Maybe I can go next time."

"They have viewings every week." He waves his arm excitedly. "Of course, I can only go when someone drives me. Ooh, maybe one of your parents can take us this week!"

"I don't know about that." I look down, tugging at the fringe of a faded maroon throw pillow. "There's something major I found out a week ago."

"What is it?" He climbs onto the other end of the sofa and perches there, completely focused on me.

I take a deep breath. "I think...I'm adopted."

Ig's eyes practically bug out of his head. "W-what?"

"That genetics assignment? My mother was way against the whole idea from the second I explained about it. Didn't want to help at all. Then my parents kept arguing about whether or not I should even do the assignment. So I decided I'd just have to get it done on my own. I went into the attic to search for family records. Instead, I found this."

I hand him the envelope with the duck birthday card and picture. Thank goodness Mami's purse was waterproof.

"W. D. Martin," he reads off of the envelope. He looks inside the card and frowns. "But...who're Wilson and Renee?"

"That's just it. I don't remember anyone by those names. And it seems like my parents went out of their way to make sure I never did."

He examines the card again. "And you think this Wilson and Renee are your...your real parents? Biological, I mean.'"

I nod. "She's not even in the picture." A lump forms in my throat. "So if I really am adopted, I have no clue what my real, I mean, birth mother even looks like." I wipe away tears, not caring anymore if Ig sees them. "It's like, I don't even know the whole truth of me. Just bits and pieces." I twist the pillow, as if strangling it will help. "What if I am adopted and my birth parents are totally different than my family? What if I'd known about it this whole time? And, I mean, *why* haven't I known? There's no escaping your genes, right? So, what if—"

"Hey, wait." He takes hold of the pillow, stopping me from busting a seam. "That's a whole lot of what-ifs."

"Exactly!" I throw my arms up, exasperated. "How can I be the real me without knowing all the cold hard facts?"

"Yeah. I get it." Ig hands back the envelope with a sad look. "It's hard. Not knowing about your past."

"Right. I guess I don't have to tell you that." It hasn't dawned on me until now. This same uncertainty, Ig's had it about his father his entire life. "Part of me wishes everything could go back to how it used to be. Before I found the envelope. Before the genetics project. Can you believe a simple homework assignment could ruin both our lives?"

"I don't know." He tilts his head to one side, considering. "When you think about it, even if the project had never happened, we'd still need to deal with this stuff sooner or later."

I can't believe what I'm hearing. Is this the same Ig who was so angry about the Blueprint of Life project? "Well, I wish we didn't have to deal with it. Not ever! That there were no family mysteries. No questions. No secrets."

"But it seems like you might be able to solve your mystery," he points out. "Or at least part of it."

I nod then. Because I'd already been thinking the same thing. I just have to talk with my parents and demand the truth.

I lean my head back on the sofa. My life feels super complicated now. But at least I know I can count on Ig again. I'm going to need his calm and logic, with all this family drama about to explode. And maybe he needs me too.

Out of nowhere, footsteps thump overhead. The door to the basement flies open. Ms. Soto runs down, holding a cell phone to her ear. When she sees me, she stops dead and gasps, "*Gracias a Dios.* Oscar, she's right here!"

CHAPTER EIGHTEEN:
THE TRUTH

Ms. Soto starts backing out of our driveway as soon as Papi waves from the front door that he's holding open for me. I walk inside and it feels like I'm stepping into yet another life, about to learn the whole truth about my past. Finally, I'm ready to hear it.

My mother hugs me hard with what seems like both relief and anger. "I called Sara's house. She said you left over two hours ago. *Ay,* your hair's soaked!"

"It's raining."

She tugs at the shirt. "And these *clothes.*"

"Ig leant them to me." I drop the bags with my own sodden outfit. "Mine got wet."

"And how'd you get over to Ignacio's house?" My father's arms are crossed, his voice so stern I'm afraid to look him in the eye.

"Walked," I whisper.

He takes a deep breath. Puts his hands up on the back of his head, and stares at the ceiling a moment. "You will not scare us like that again. Ever. Do you understand?"

I nod, clasping my own hands together to stop their shaking. I kick off my boots—well, my mother's boots, also soaked.

She doesn't seem to notice, or even care that I borrowed them without asking. "You should've told us where you were going." She motions for me to follow them into the living room. Papi sits on the edge of the burgundy loveseat, leaning forward, massaging his temples. Mami drops next to him and puts a hand on his back. They seem really intense. Then it hits me: This is as huge a moment for them as it is for me.

I take a seat on the sofa, across.

"We need to talk, about..." Mami's voice trails off.

"I know what it's about," I say.

My parents glance at each other but say nothing.

"At least, I think I do. I found an envelope in your old trunk."

"What?" Mami shakes her head. "The one in the attic?"

"There was a name." I lower my eyes. "Wilson Martin."

"Yes," she whispers, nodding. "Wilson."

I hug my knees. "In the picture it was only him. The woman wasn't there."

"Woman?" They ask in unison, giving each other more looks. Confused this time.

Mami stares at me. "Justina, who are you talking about?"

"A woman named Renee." I jump up. "I can't believe you're *still* not going to tell me the truth! Don't you think I know what's going on? That I deserve to know about the woman who gave birth to me."

My mother gasps. Papi mumbles. *"Ay Dios."*

"Unless...unless you guys don't actually know who she is." *Ay Dios*, indeed. Why hadn't this possibility crossed my mind until now? I fall back onto the sofa, stunned.

Next thing I know they're both sitting on either side of me. Mami grabs my right hand, eyes welling up. *"I gave birth to you. And I'm so sorry I ever made you doubt that."* She hugs me tight and then my tears flow too. Because I know she's telling the truth. I'd known it already, deep in my DNA.

But still, Papi is watching with a hand covering his mouth, and I can't forget there are still so many unanswered questions. The clues that don't add up. I lean back and ask, "But then who's Wilson Martin?"

"Mar-TEEN." Mami says his name the Spanish way. The right way. "His parents are from Puerto Rico."

"Martín," I repeat. I'd just assumed it was the Anglo version of that last name, but I was wrong.

My mother nods, sliding her wedding band up and down, to the knuckle and back. "You see, I studied in Puerto Rico for my final semester of grad school. Wilson was in a class with me studying Taino art. We both stayed with family on the island. We had that in common." She takes a deep breath. "Well. We started a...a relationship. He was a little older. Neither of us intended it to be more than a summer romance. But by the end of the semester, well...I learned I was pregnant with you."

The cold hard facts pour in like a flash flood, so fast my brain can hardly keep up. I need my notebook. I need my *coquí*. I need...my parents. They hold me as I sob.

"Your mother and I had already dated on and off before that summer," Papi says. "When I found out the situation, I asked her to marry me. I told her I wanted to raise you as my own daughter. And of course we made it official through the legal system. I adopted you when you were a baby."

My entire body is trembling now. The man who doesn't share any of my DNA keeps me upright when it feels like all my bones have turned to liquid. "You're *my* girl," he whispers. *"Mi niña."*

And it's true. I am. I've always been. Papi said it: *I am his.*

But then what about Wilson? "But the card I found. I mean, did this Wilson guy just decide after my first birthday to forget all about me?" My voice has an edge to it I hadn't intended.

"No, that's not how it was at all," Mami whispers. "Wilson...he loved you." She looks at the ceiling fan, blinking hard and fast. "When I told him I was pregnant, back then, he let me know he was still married."

"Married? To Renee?"

She nods. "See, they were separated at the time, and so...well, never mind all that. At first he tried to stay in touch. Sent cards and money. But Papi and I didn't want you to feel rejected or abandoned because of the circumstances. So we decided it'd be less confusing if...if..."

"So you didn't tell me."

"We see now how wrong it was to break off contact with him," Mami says, looking down at her lap and sighing.

Papi turns to me. "It's absolutely understandable if all of this upsets you. Even if you are angry at us."

I'm too exhausted to know how I really feel. Shocked, but relieved. Confused, but comforted. Betrayed, but loved. I wipe away more tears.

"We thought we were protecting you." Mami's arm tightens around my shoulder. "That as long as we kept you happy, you didn't need to know about Wilson. And it seemed to work for a long time. But then you were assigned the genetics project."

"What if that had never happened?" I ask. "Would you have kept it from me forever?"

They eye each other as if trying to find the proper, the best thing to say. Finally, Papi speaks. "We felt we had to find the perfect time. The perfect way to tell you."

My heart speeds up. "Do you know where Wilson is now?"

Mami sounds unsure. "Last I heard, living in Connecticut."

"Not anymore," I say.

They both seem shocked then.

Papi clears his throat. "Why do you say that?"

"I've done some research." It's only right to admit what I've learned using my detective skills. From now on, no more secrets in this family.

CHAPTER NINETEEN:
QUESTIONS

The next morning I snuggle my quilt up to my chin, so comfy I could sleep for hours.

There's a knock at the door.

"Mmmh..." I turn away and bury my face in the pillow.

My mother enters the room. "Ignacio's downstairs."

I force my eyes open. "What's he doing here so early?"

"It's close to lunch time."

I flop up and scratch my head. "Let me get cleaned up."

Mami heads back downstairs. I twist my hair into a messy ponytail. In the bathroom, my face looks an even bigger mess. Eyes red, like I've had an allergic reaction, only it's from all the crying last night. I quickly wash my face and brush my teeth, then shout from the top of the stairs, "Ig, come on up."

He follows me into my room and we lounge on the floor as if we're back in our corner of the school library, about to start a meeting. He makes a face. "Lah made me have fake Japanese tea with that weird doll she talks to."

I roll my eyes. "Now you know what I have to put up with every Tuesday and Thursday afternoon."

He smiles and hands me a worn paperback copy of *The Westing Game*. "Look what I found this morning."

I open the cover. There's a stamp of a kitten holding up a sign that reads—THIS BOOK BELONGS TO—and underneath, my name carefully printed in all caps. "I haven't seen this in over a year. Where was it?"

"My mother made me clean every inch of my room," Ig says. "Punishment for not telling her you'd shown up at our house in the middle of the night."

"Oh." I toss the book up on the nightstand next to me. "Sorry."

He shrugs. "It's not like I was gonna leave you standing out in the rain. How you doing?"

I yank up the tube socks he gave me the night before. "Turns out I was right, and wrong."

As I tell Ig everything, he listens, nodding, grabbing me tissues from my nightstand when I get to the part about Papi holding me. After I'm done, I rest my head on his shoulder. We sit in silence until I fall asleep again.

When I wake, he's still there, reading the third chapter of *The Westing Game*.

"You never snored when we took naps in daycare." He lays the book on the floor.

"Liar." I straighten up and stretch. "I don't snore."

His eyebrows rise. "Yeah, you do. Like a car engine that needs fixing."

"Ha! You should hear Papi. That's probably where I get it from. I mean..." I pick at my nails, feeling my face heat up. "What a stupid thing to say, huh?"

"Hey." Ig smiles. "You could've gotten it from him. Like, learned behavior, right?"

"Maybe. I wonder if Wilson Martín snores."

Ig's silent for a moment. Then he asks, "You think you...maybe want to meet him?"

I pause, wondering. "My mother told me she still has a few old phone numbers for his family in Puerto Rico. She said she'd call and try to track him down. And if we do find him, well, I guess I'll decide then. I mean, when and how I want to meet him."

Just then Lah takes a running leap from the doorway to land on my bed. She crawls over and sits, playing with my ponytail. "I like her hair better this way. Don't you, Ig?"

He laughs. "Yeah. I do."

* * *

In front of the computer screen in Papi's office, I glance up at the clay Maltese Falcon sculpture, back in its spot on the desk shelf. It's easy to see the line where he stuck it back together with my mother's hot glue gun. Once he'd finished, he stepped back and tilted his head. "I like it even better now. It's got character."

Now, I tug at my *coquí* necklace, also back in its proper place, around my neck. Mami is behind me, trying to break the world record for nervous pacing. She hasn't stopped since I started doing web searches of the list of names she dictated while I wrote in the back of my casebook:

PEOPLE AND PLACES TO SEARCH:
- Wilson Martín (father)
- Ida and Perdo Martín (grandparents)
- Lolo Martín (uncle)
- Aurora (aunt, last name unknown)
- Carolina, Puerto Rico (town where grandparents lived)
- Lindon, Connecticut (where Wilson lived/lives?)
- Rutgers University (where Wilson went to college)

I've tried one combination after another, but I can't find my Martín family in Puerto Rico. Nothing has led me to Wilson Martín in the states either. After scanning dozens of pages of search results, I finally click on a link to Wilson Diego Martín in Jersey City. Up pops a picture of a man with a receding hairline—what's left is a mix of gray and dirty blond. I leap from the desk chair when I see his amber eyes. "Hey! I think I found him."

"You did?" Mami rushes up behind me. "Oh yes. That's him, all right. And there's his number. Now, I can call him." She steps back from the computer desk and lets out a long-held breath. "If you're ready, that is."

I start to pace just like her. Now that we've found the mysterious Wilson Martín and meeting him is a real possibility, it makes me super nervous. I guess this thing could go so many ways. And I can't control it. But finding out is what I've wanted all along. A chance to uncover the mystery of my past. Still, what if I get the cold hard facts and don't like them? Maybe it's safer to stick to what I know.

I look at Mami, trembling and terrified. But she's clearly ready to take this huge step for me, if it's what I want.

At last, I place a hand on my *coquí* charm and take a deep breath. "Go ahead. But if he asks to talk to me, I...tell him, not yet. I mean, the first time we say anything to each other, I want it to be in person."

"Does this mean you want to meet him...soon?" She tucks a lock of hair behind my ear.

I nod. "I think so. Yeah, I really do."

She dials the number and puts the phone on speaker. Then both of us pace, in opposite directions. When a man's voice answers, she stops suddenly. Her eyes grow wide. "W-wilson?" She clears her throat. "It's...Alana."

I listen with every cell in my body.

"My God," the deep voice rumbles. "Alana! Is it really you?"

"Yeah, it's me." She blinks hard.

"How are you? How's little Justina?" He says my name the Spanish way. The right way.

I collapse into the office chair. Oh. My. God.

"She's incredible." Mami smiles and tears roll down her cheeks. "But not so little now. And... she wants to meet you."

CHAPTER TWENTY:
NEW DEVELOPMENTS

On Monday, I'm the first one to arrive in health class. Mrs. Mollick is organizing the dry-erase markers for the white board. She smiles when she sees my sunny yellow cardigan, hand-knitted by Titi Nessa. "Morning, Justina! Good to see you back to your old self."

"Thanks," I say. "Um, I know the genetics project is due tomorrow. But I was wondering if there's any way to receive partial credit if I have to hand it in late?"

"Late?" Her smile dims. "But why?"

I place one hand on her desk as if I'm a lawyer asking the court judge to consider a client's situation. "Circumstances beyond my control that've led to, well, some new evidence. It's almost like I have to start my investigation over again. I'll explain it all in my report."

At last she nods. "I'll give you another week. But that's all."

"Thanks." I take my seat, relieved to have the extra time. And a little embarrassed, because I've never handed anything in late before.

Ig rushes through the door and throws himself into the desk next to mine. "Sara just told me there's been another backstage incident," he whispers. "More vandalism, only with a different name."

"What!" I didn't see this coming. "Whose?"

"Ayesha."

The bell rings, Mrs. Mollick makes an announcement. "We've just found out this morning that construction will begin next week in the library. The librarian will be working out of the new conference room where there'll be a temporary check-out desk and computer lab for at least six weeks."

My gaze meets Ig's. *At least six weeks?* Sounds like the Seventh-Grade Sleuths will have to find a temporary spot to meet. Even if it's just the two of us. Who knows if Gunther still wants to be part of the club after I swore off mysteries and then fled from Sara's party.

Mrs. Mollick starts taking attendance.

I flip open the case notebook. Right under my scrawling about Franklin I jot down the new details about Ayesha.

FRANKLIN: Not a current suspect
- Plays "Sir Serious"
- Perfectionist who never stops rehearsing the play
- Acceptance to arts magnet high school depends on this production

AYESHA: Not a current suspect, second victim!!!
- Plays "The Jester"
- Sara's best friend

SERIOUSLAND

CAST LIST:
Lady Luciana—Sara Baker
Sir Serious—Franklin Diaz
The Jester—Ayesha Malloy
The Servant—Janine Petite
The Beggar—Elizabeth Moore
The Prince—Raj Gupta
Female Understudy—Nina Minchi
Male Understudy—Seth Bernstein

Set Construction/Tech Crew:
Seth Bernstein, Gunther Corrie, Nina Minchi, Elijah Roberts

"Well, that confirms it," I say to Ig, closing the casebook. "We've run out of suspects."

He sighs. "Now what?"

I sigh too. "Maybe we'll never catch the vandal."

It's a cold hard fact, you know. Some cases are never solved.

CHAPTER TWENTY-ONE:
ANSWERS

"Here we go. Visitor's parking." Titi Nessa pulls her car into an underground parking spot beneath a high-rise building in Jersey City. She offered to be the one to come along once she found out I was going to meet Wilson. "Because I'm neutral," she'd pointed out. "Unbiased." Like we were going to the United Nations to sign an international treaty or something.

We climb out of the car and follow a brick staircase leading to a fancy lobby with tall windows and a marble-tiled floor. The man behind the front desk asks us to sign in, confirms Wilson's apartment number, and tells us to take the elevator to the tenth floor.

"Ready?" Titi asks in a low, soothing counselor's voice, when the elevator door opens.

I nod, relieved we're the only ones stepping in. I watch each number light up, thinking how only a few weeks ago I had no idea there was a man named Wilson Martín. No idea that for twelve years, my parents held onto a secret they thought was too painful for me to deal with. Now, I'm about to meet my biological father.

The elevator door slides open. We step out into a hallway of mirrored walls that makes it seem like there are an infinite number of apartments on either side. I take a deep breath. "Okay." I smile. "Let's go."

When we reach his apartment number, Titi Nessa rings the doorbell.

Footsteps thump up to the other side of the door. But for a few seconds nothing happens. Maybe Wilson needs to breathe a little first, too? At last, the deadbolt clicks. The knob turns. Finally, the door swings open.

"Justina?" He looks like his picture. Same hair. Same eyes.

I nod slowly. But what should I call him? Wilson? Mr. Martín? Surely not...Papi. I already have one of those.

"Come on in." He shakes Titi's hand as she enters. "I'm Wilson."

"Vanessa," she says. "So nice to meet you."

Wilson stares at me. "Your mother's right. You are beautiful."

I turn my gaze to a stone sculpture in one corner of the small foyer, feeling a bit embarrassed and proud at the same time. "Oh, she tells everyone that."

"Well, and why not?" He smiles. "It's true."

I shuffle my feet, wondering if he thinks my painted-butterfly Mary Jane shoes are weird. "Uh, thanks."

He leads us into a family room full of artwork. A pair of African tribal figures. Puppets, maybe? There's also a series of framed symbols. Taino, I think. That is what he and Mami studied all those years ago. The image farthest away is similar to the *coquí* hanging on a chain around my neck. I tug on the necklace.

Wilson notices. "That charm—"

"It was my grandmother's."

He opens his mouth as if about to tell me something. Then just shakes his head as if to say, Never mind. He points to a pitcher on a tray. "Lemonade?"

Titi and I both say yes. He hands us each a full glass. I've never tasted such cool, refreshing lemonade in my life. I take a seat next to my aunt on the edge of an antique sofa. Wilson sits across from us in a matching armchair.

"What a great room." Titi Nessa looks around. "The artwork, the furniture."

"Oh, thanks. Got the antiquing bug. And, in case you didn't figure it out yet, I collect indigenous art from the Caribbean." He turns to me, rubbing his chin. "What about you? Any hobbies?"

"Well." I lean back a little, trying to get comfortable. "Mystery stories and films. Especially old ones. And I'm good at playing dominoes." I don't even care if it sounds like I'm bragging. "I usually win."

He laughs. "My mother—your grandmother—is a dominoes shark. Every night she's on her porch beating the socks off the neighbors."

He opens a photo album and shows me a picture of an older woman standing in front of a flower garden. Her skin is a golden tan. Her hair's pulled into a low bun. "That's her."

I blink hard. *She's* wearing the necklace. So that's why he started to say something before but stopped himself. My necklace, it once belonged to her! My other grandmother. The one I don't know yet.

Wilson points to another picture, a faded image of a young boy with pale skin and bright golden curls. "That's me when I was a kid. See—lots more hair then."

On the opposite page there's a photo of a beautiful woman with cocoa-colored skin whose face I've seen before. But where?

He must notice me eyeing it because he quietly says, "That was Renee, my wife. She died four years ago."

"Oh. S-sorry." I shift in my seat, not sure what to say next.

Wilson leans his forearms on his thighs. "I know all this is new, and hard to talk about. But I want you to understand things weren't as simple as..." He takes a deep breath. "Back then, Renee and I were close to getting a divorce. We'd been separated for a while when I met Alana." He says Mami's name with a gentle smile. I can tell he really cared for her. "Your mother probably doesn't know how much she helped me through...a complicated time."

It's strange to hear all this major stuff about her that happened before I was even born. Especially since there are still gaps in the story. And a huge question still hasn't been answered.

Why didn't Wilson stay with Mami if she was such an important part of his life?

Titi Nessa holds my hand. "You okay, *m'ija?*"

"Yeah." My turn to take a deep breath. "But I don't understand...I mean, after that summer, why..." But I can't bring myself to ask, Why did you leave us?

Instead, I state it. The cold hard fact: "You got back together with your wife."

He nods. "Something unexpected made us reconsider."

A door slams. A girl my age runs into the room. Shorter than me, but with curls just like mine. Only hers are jet black and swept up into a messy ponytail with a few wispy locks framing her mahogany face.

She tosses a duffle bag on an armchair. "Sorry I'm late. I was supposed to be here when you arrived but gymnastics practice went way long. And then the PATH train took forever to come."

Then she glances at me and, for a second, there's a strange look in her eyes. I can't tell what it is exactly.

152

Judgment? Jealousy? But just like that, it's gone. She's grinning as if she's known me since daycare. "Hey! We so have the same hair. Nightmare, right?"

I reach up to touch my own curls, utterly confused by the whirlwind entrance. "Um, yeah." That's all I manage to say because my brain hasn't caught up to what my gut is telling me: this girl is too familiar to be a true stranger.

"Blame him." She points to Wilson. "Frizzy Martín."

He clears his throat. "Justina, this is Allie. Your half-sister."

I glance at Titi, whose mouth is hanging open. Then turn back to this bizarre, bouncy newcomer. And my brain finally understands that things are even more complicated than I had ever imagined.

CHAPTER TWENTY-TWO:
ALLIE

A llie's a talker. I've only known her a few minutes and have already learned she's a level-nine gymnast, on the school council, and her mom was a respected artist and professor at a prestigious art institute. Once she told me that, I finally remembered where I'd seen her mother's face before. One of the many Renee Martíns that had shown up during my online research sessions. The African-American puppeteer.

Allie always knew the truth about me. Like, her whole life. Wilson and Allie don't seem to have kept secrets from each other. Meanwhile, my family suffered fighting over schoolwork, two ruined outings, a dramatic makeover, a lame runaway attempt—before my parents would even tell me the cold hard facts.

"You were totally right, Pa." Allie is picking at a patch of callused skin in the center of her palm. "We just had to be patient and we'd get to meet her when the time was right."

And when she says this, the world doesn't shatter or blow up or anything.

Wilson just nods. "True. Now sweetheart, could you please leave hand maintenance until after the company leaves? It's sort of—"

"Sorry. I got a rip during workout today." She holds the hand out to show me and Titi. There's a purplish-pink spot with a white semi-circular flap of skin sticking straight up, directly under the middle finger. "Gross, right?"

"Allison." Wilson sighs and clicks his tongue. "Really."

It is pretty gross. But I laugh because Allie's so different from Lah, who's mostly worried about things being pretty, and teaching me proper Tea Time etiquette.

"You must be thirsty from all that exercising." Titi lifts the pitcher of lemonade, ready to pour a glass for Allie. As if her way of dealing with shock is to play hostess even when she's in someone else's home. "Want some?"

"*Gracias.*" Allie wrinkles her nose. "*Pero no me gusta.* I could go for some coffee, though."

155

"Decaf, at this hour," warns Wilson.

She rolls her eyes. *"Claro,* Pa."

So here's this girl, who's half African-American, speaking Spanish more fluently and comfortably than I do.

"You drink it?" she asks.

I nod. "I love coffee."

"We're so sisters." She grins and holds up a hand, the one that isn't shedding skin. It's weird giving her a high five since we only just met, but I do anyway. "Come on." She goes to the doorway leading further into the apartment.

Titi winks at me. "Go on!"

I follow Allie into the kitchen, which smells like the pine stuff my parents also use to mop the floors. She opens a cabinet with a swirly black knob and grabs a tin of Café Bustelo. It has the green 'decaf' band around the bottom. She pops off the lid. Ah, there's nothing like the strong smell of coffee to put me at ease.

"Are you fluent?" I ask.

"In Spanish?" Allie shrugs, then pours filtered tap water into the bottom of a stovetop coffee maker. She scoops coffee into the metal basket. "I know enough to make it through a conversation. But if you do anything with confidence, people'll buy it."

She turns on the burner. "Do me a favor and get the milk from the fridge?"

I laugh. "It's just like being in the kitchen with my mother," I say, then freeze, hiding my wincing face behind the fridge door. "Um, ignore what I just said."

"You can talk about your mom." Allie takes the carton from me with a huge smile. Almost too huge. Part of me wonders if she's forcing it. "My mother actually wanted you to be part of our lives. She was totally okay with how it all happened." Her smile starts to fade. "Kinda had to be, since she was the one who'd asked for the divorce. Anyhow, she didn't think she'd live as long as she did. And she definitely didn't expect me to come along."

Allie's smile is totally gone now. We stand in silence, the fridge door between us. That look in her eyes is back, the one she got when she first saw me. I realize what it is now, because I've been there too. That weight of knowing her place in her father's life wasn't exactly what she'd believed.

I want her to know I'm not trying to come between them. "You and your father seem really close."

She considers that a moment, then smiles, not as huge as before. But a real grin. "We've always been. Especially since it's been only us the past few years."

"Papi and I are close, too," I lean against the counter. "He gets really busy with work now, though. And my little sister is always trying to steal him for her fake tea parties. But we still spend time together, usually watching old black and white movies. Weird, right?"

"No. I don't think so. Sounds kind of fun." Allie pulls out an elastic to let down her thick hair. "You ever just want to cut all this hair off?"

"No," I say. "But I did dye it brown once."

Wilson strolls into the kitchen then. Titi Nessa comes to stand in the doorway.

"Really?" Allie reaches for pottery mugs in the cabinet and sets them on the counter. "But I love your color. Pa's hair used to be just like that. I get it though. Sometimes I get sick of having black hair."

Wilson puts the empty lemonade pitcher in the sink and gazes at us both, smiling. "Your grandmother always used to talk about changing her hair. Must run in the family."

Allie grabs a tin container of sugar. "I hope that also means I inherited her talent for making delicious desserts." She turns to me. "Abuela makes the *best* rice pudding. To die for! I swear, my coaches hate when we visit family in Puerto Rico because I always gain five pounds."

I remember the stack of dessert recipes then and finally understand—the pocket in the back of the trunk is where Mami stashed away all she had left of Wilson and his family. The recipes. The *coquí* necklace. The birthday card. The picture. Deep down inside, she must've known she'd been keeping them for me all this time.

"Sounds like you'll need to take a trip to Puerto Rico to taste your grandmother's desserts, Justina," my aunt says.

"Yeah." I tap the *coquí* charm that I now know once belonged to her. "And to show her this."

CHAPTER TWENTY-THREE:
CASE CLOSED

It's the start of another week, and an entire month since our mystery club began trying to solve the Case of the Backstage Vandal. We should've nabbed the culprit by now. But then, we did have some major detours along the way.

Ig and I sit at our regular spots in the cafetorium. It seems extra-loud in here today. Maybe everyone's pumped about the Fall Festival tonight. Even Ig admitted he's excited to show off his discoveries about his mother's side of the family. Of course, I won't take part in the festival because I'm still working on my project. But I'm fine with that, especially since Mami and Wilson have both been helping me find more genetic evidence. Now, it's like this assignment is for me as much as for a grade in Health Studies.

Ig shakes his head, staring at the table behind me. "I just don't get them."

"Who?" I turn to look.

At the next table Sara and Janine are trying to paint pictures on their skin using red nail polish. Gunther sneaks behind them and snatches the little bottle.

"Hey! I'm not done with my design yet," Janine yells.

"Isn't this stuff for nails?" Gunther smirks as he reads off the label. "Shades of Eve: All-Natural Nail Color. *Ooooh.*"

"Yeah, organic nail polish. My sister paid a lot of money for that. So you better not—" Sara lunges for it with one hand but misses. "Gunther Corrie. You're dead if this smears."

Ig rolls his eyes. "At least now we don't need to deal with Sara's backstage drama."

"Actually." I grab the casebook from my messenger bag. "We're still on the case."

He looks surprised. "But we're out of suspects."

"Not quite. We've only investigated the cast and crew. But what do we know about the adults involved?" I flip open to the suspect list. "I mean, I don't really know anything about Mr. Vincent. And how about the hundreds of students who aren't *in* the school play? They all had access, too."

Ig lets his head fall back, groaning. "We can't interview everyone in the whole school."

"You're right." I nod. "That's why we need to revisit the scene of the crime for a closer inspection. Maybe there's something we're missing. Does the vandal have a grudge against Sara and Ayesha or the entire drama club? How about all the students who auditioned but weren't cast in the show. That could be a motive."

"Please." Ig holds up a hand. "That's a lot of scheming for a part in one little middle school play."

"Well, it is the *drama* club." I smile sweetly at him. "Anyhow, we should solve this case. That's what good detectives do, Ig. You know that."

He raises his eyebrows like he knows what I'm about to ask.

"So maybe after school we could go backstage to investigate?" I give him big amber puppy-dog eyes. "Don't leave me to face an angry ghost or crazed lunatic all by myself."

Ig laughs. "So you believe one of the teachers has something against Sara Baker and Ayesha Malloy?"

"Okay, maybe not. But you should still come."

He throws his head back again, but now I detect a slight grin. "Okay. Fine."

"Your eyes will adjust to the dark," I tell Ig later.

Only a few minutes have passed since the final bell of the day. We climb the steps from the side entrance in the cafetorium onto the stage. We must work quickly, before the cast shows up for rehearsal. I follow the dim

162

yellow light that slips through the maze of curtains and costumes until we reached the prop table. Behind it are two pieces of foam-board scenery. One with Sara's name carved into it, the other with Ayesha's.

I haul out the shoebox with foam scraps Sara had saved, still tucked behind the wastebasket. "There must be a reason the vandal left behind these uneven chunks."

There's a rustling behind the costume racks. We both freeze. Is it a maniac? A vengeful ghost? A—

Someone runs out from behind a long black curtain. "AHHHHHHHHH!"

Ig and I clutch at each other. I scream, expecting to meet a horrible, bloody fate. Until we realize it's only Gunther. He jumps onto a large wooden throne, a set piece. And since he looks genuinely terrified, we both hop up to huddle on either side of him.

"What is it? Is someone following you?" I whisper. "Are they brandishing a weapon?"

Ig eyes me like I'm even nuttier than Gunther. "Brandishing a weapon?"

"Shhh!" I hold up a hand for silence. "Let him—"

But Gunther's still not able to form words. "M-m-m-m-m—"

I quickly run through the cast and crew list in my mind. "Minchi? Nina Minchi? Is she armed with sewing needles or...*a seam ripper?*"

He shakes his head. "No! M-m-m—"

163

"Moore, Liz?" He shakes his head. I keep on guessing. "Malloy, Ayesha? But she's—"

With one trembling finger, he points to the bottom of the curtain he just burst through.

"Monster?" I shudder at the thought.

Just then, there's a tiny squeak from beneath the curtain.

"YAH-ACK-EEK!" Gunther covers his eyes. "Get it...get it..."

Ig grabs his shoulders and shakes them a little. "Spit it out, dude."

A little gray mouse creeps from underneath the black curtain.

"Oh. It's just a *mouse.*" I hop back down onto the stage floor and it scurries underneath the prop table.

"Geez." Ig drops his arms by his sides. "You'd think a freaking werewolf was about to attack."

I cross my arms and glare at Prince Scaredy-Cat. "It's gone, Gunther."

"The school said the mice were all *taken care of!* Wait until my father hears about this." He climbs down slowly, warily, like he's expecting the killer mouse to run out any second, bare huge fangs, and bite a chunk out of him. I set the shoebox back in its hiding place. That's when I notice an empty tube of lip balm lying in the bottom of the trash bin. Using a rag from the prop table, so as not to leave any fingerprints, I fish it out to inspect the label. All-Natural Pomegranate-flavored Lip Balm.

All-Natural. Pomegranate. Lip Balm.

"Of course." I slide the foam fake shrub from behind the prop table and sniff at the area with Sara's name. "Ah ha. Just as I suspected. Fruity."

Ig seems impressed. "You mean—you know who did it?"

"Not exactly *who.*"

There's another squeak from underneath the prop table.

Gunther jumps on the throne again. "Ew, ew! Did you hear that beast?"

The mouse comes out again, carrying a tiny chunk of light blue foam in its mouth.

I turn back to my fellow seventh-grade detectives. "But I know *what* did it."

"The mouse?" Gunther shouts, which seems to scare the furry little creature. It darts back under the prop table.

Ig slaps a hand to his forehead like it all makes perfect sense now.

Gunther frowns. "Wait a minute. How could a mouse write a name?"

I sigh. "Obviously, Sara and Ayesha wrote their own names. With the lip balm. The mouse only nibbled away the all-natural, fruit-flavored outline."

"So...this all happened because those two can't stop using make-up and nail polish as art supplies?" Gunther says from his high perch, as if it's all been solved thanks to him.

Ig raises his eyebrows. "Does this little get-together count as our mystery club meeting today?"

"That depends." Gunther stares at me. "Are we *still* the Seventh-Grade Sleuths?"

True, only a little over a week ago, at Sara's party, I'd sworn off mysteries. But so much has changed since then. Only Gunther doesn't really have a clue about all that. I know now he'll never understand me like my best friend since daycare. "Of course we are. Maybe we should find more real-life cases to solve."

Ig nods. "Yeah!"

"OK, I'm in." Gunther jumps off the majestic fake throne. "But from now on, let's go for ones that don't involve—"

Someone coughs behind us. "Excuse me, but this can't be your new meeting spot." Sara's standing a few feet away, hands on her hips. "I mean, I know right now the library's out, but you guys can't just show up backstage whenever you want. And Ms. Lee will be here any minute. I can't let her see this!" She yanks the foam board out of my hand.

Maybe Sara's still upset about the way I left her party. But it's not like she owns the stage. I cross my arms. "How about a thank-you for solving the case?"

"You know who did it?" A smile creeps across her face. "Wait until I get my hands on the jerk."

"Good luck with that," Ig says. He and Gunther crack up.

Sara scowls. "What's so funny?"

166

"The culprit?" I shake my head. "It was a mouse."

"Huh?" She squints and screws up her mouth like she just tasted dirt. "What's a culprit?"

"Take a sniff right where your name is." I point to the middle of the foam board. She hesitates, but then does as she's told, for a change. "It was a mouse who likes the taste of organic pomegranate lip balm." I plop the tube of gloss into her hand.

"So...no one is actually trying to take me down?" She frowns at the tube a moment, and then her face brightens. "See, I just knew it. Everyone in my cast and crew is such a sweetheart. The most supportive bunch you've ever met."

"Really?" I look to Ig and Gunther, who are both smirking. "Even Nina Minchi?"

"Especially Nina! I mean, she made me this lovely costume." Sara dashes to the wardrobe rack, holds up her bodice and skirt, and twirls out to center stage. "I couldn't do this role without Nina."

I roll my eyes. "Let's leave Sara to her fantasy world."

The three of us exit stage right, out into the cafetorium.

I spend the rest of the school week wondering if the construction crew is going to get rid of our secret alcove meeting spot in the library. But then I come up with the idea to have our mystery club meetings at my home during the weekend. And that's how the three of us end up sprawled out in my father's office on a Saturday evening. We've just finished dinner. Gunther and Ig weren't shy about asking for seconds of my mother's stewed chicken with white rice, red beans, and sweet plantains.

"Oh man. Will we get a meal like that every Saturday?" Gunther lies back on the light brown carpet, patting his stomach. "Because I'll never skip a meeting. Ever."

Ig snorts. "First time eating Puerto Rican food, dude?"

"I had no clue what I was missing." Gunther shakes his head.

We all laugh. Finally, I say, "Okay. Time to get down to business."

I grab a couple of notebooks from my messenger bag and hand one each to Ig and Gunther. "Time you guys had your own casebooks." I hold up the one I've been using all along. "I'm officially claiming this as mine." I flip open to the page where I've added the final notes on the Case of the Backstage Vandal:

CULPRIT: Hungry backstage mouse
CASE CLOSED

Gunther sighs. "What we need is a new case. With taller criminals."

"Right." I nod. "We'll have to be on the lookout for one. Use our observation skills. Life's full of mysteries."

I should know.

Just then a computer alarm sounds. A request to video chat.

"Oh, I forgot! My sister wanted to video chat after she got home from gymnastics practice."

"Your sister?" Gunther scratches his head. "Wasn't she at dinner with us?"

"I also have a half-sister in Jersey City. Long story. I'll fill you in later." I rush to the screen and accept the call. "Hey, Allie."

"Hey, Ju!" She pops up on the screen. "Whoa, you didn't tell me you were having a party."

"Not a party. Just a meeting. Did I forget to tell you I'm in a club that solves mysteries?"

"Mysteries?" She smiles. "Cool."

Ig clears his throat. "We're the Seventh-Grade Sleuths."

"Uh...this is Ig and Gunther." I point to them. "Guys, my half-sister, Allie."

There's a chorus of hellos followed by an awkward silence.

"Guess I should call back later. Unless..." Allie leans in so her pretty brown face appears huge on the screen. "I'm kind of curious about what sleuths do. Mind if I listen in?"

Gunther stares at the screen with the goofiest grin on his face. "Why not join?"

169

Ig's eyebrows make two high arches, letting me know I'm not the only one who's surprised by Gunther's unexpected invitation. I mean, I wouldn't be against it, but Allie doesn't even go to school with us. And besides, she's always at the gym.

"Hmm. My gymnastics schedule's pretty busy." She actually looks really interested. "But I usually have Saturday nights off, except for competition season. Hey, maybe it could work if I can video chat like this for some meetings."

Gunther shrugs. "I'm fine with that."

"Me too," Ig says.

The guys both turn to me.

"Of course, I'm cool with it. She's *my* sister!" I turn to the screen, smiling. "Allie, welcome to the club."

CHAPTER TWENTY-FOUR:
PROOF

The next morning I'm standing in the doorway of Lah's room with my eyes squeezed shut.

"No peeking," she cries.

"I'm not."

I hear clinks and scrapes as she shifts things around on her Tea Time table. "Okay, done. You can look now."

I open my eyes. There on the table is a toy espresso set and Papi's designer dominoes—the ones with the Puerto Rican flag on the back of each tile. Lah's grinning, hugging Delilah Juniorette. Both she and the doll are dressed in summer clothes even though it's the middle of October.

"It's Café Time," Lah announces, throwing her arms in the air dramatically. "You get to wear *chancletas.*" She holds up a pair of flip-flops. "And I asked Mami to make my hair poufy like yours."

"It's cute." Her brown waves are hugely teased and it looks totally adorable.

"Sit wherever you want," she says. "We're playing *your* way, Ju."

I slip off my socks and slide into the flip-flops, then perch on one of the tiny chairs. Lah rests Delilah Juniorette on the empty seat next to mine. She pours me a cup of pretend coffee while I shuffle the dominoes.

"You know how to play?" I ask.

"A little. Papi's been teaching me."

We each pick seven tiles and I slide the rest aside for later. The whole time Lah keeps peeking at me anxiously. I set down the double-six domino and sip air-coffee. "Check to see if you have any sixes."

She just keeps staring.

I finally ask, "What's up?"

She tilts her head to one side. "What's she like?"

"Who?" I organize my tiles from highest to lowest number of dots.

"Your new sister."

Wow. Of course. This must be a huge thing for Lah, too. One day she's my one and only sister. The next she has to share me. She probably needs exactly what I did: the cold hard facts.

"Well, uh, Allie's my age. Really nice. And she's got my kind of hair. You know, frizzy and wild, except hers is black. Oh, and she does gymnastics and—"

She looks down at her lap. "But you still want to be my sister, right?"

"Of course I do!" If only there was some way to prove I won't ever stop being her sister.

I pick up her doll from the chair next to me. "Hey, Delilah Juniorette. Guess what? I have two sisters now. I barely know Allie, though. But Lah and I were first. So we'll always have something special. Do you understand?"

Lah grabs Delilah Juniorette and holds her up to one ear. "She says she does."

I stare right into her eyes. "That's good."

"But I don't get it," Lah says. "Why'd you keep changing your hair?"

I sigh, wondering if I'll ever live that one down. "I was trying to figure out who I was."

"Oh." She nods doubtfully. "Did it work?"

"I'm getting there." I smile and take a long fake sip of pretend coffee from the tiny mug. "Hey. This is pretty good stuff!"

Later that night I'm sitting on the living room sofa, getting comfy under a maroon knit blanket, another Titi Nessa creation.

Papi presses PLAY on the television remote. *The Hound of the Baskervilles* starts just after the point where Holmes takes off his disguise. Papi stares at the screen, looking confused. "What happened?"

"It's starting where we left off last time," I say.

"Well, we can't have that." He presses menu and scrolls through the options. "Let's do this the right way. Back to the beginning."

"Remember the first time we watched this?"

He squints, thinking back. "How long's it been?"

I tilt my head. "Five years ago."

"*Ay,* how time flies," he says. "I still remember the night you were born."

I gape up at him. "You were there?"

"Sure. Wilson and I both were. You wouldn't stop crying, and neither could we. It was a real magical night." He smiles and turns off the lamp next to him.

The black and white 20th Century Fox logo of the film flashes on the screen, accompanied by a snare-drum-and-horns march. Before the opening music swells, the television goes black for a couple of seconds, leaving the room in quiet darkness. And sitting here with Papi, I've never been more certain about these cold hard facts: I am his true daughter. He is my real father. I don't need to find the evidence in my genes or secretly hidden in the attic. I already have all the proof I'll ever need.

Case closed.

Acknowledgments

My deepest gratitude to Lenore Hart, who believed in this project from the start. This book would not have been published without her mentorship, support, and editing expertise. Thank you to Northampton House Press for allowing me to share Ju with the world. My sincere thanks to David Poyer for his precise eye and pragmatic approach to publishing and writing.

I'm also indebted to many faculty members of the Wilkes University Graduate Creative Writing Program, especially Dr. Bonnie Culver, Rashidah Ismaili, Kaylie Jones, Jean Klein, Jan Quackenbush, Jeff Talarigo, and Richard Uhlig, who offered guidance and encouragement; and to Chris Tomasino, who provided a thoughtful and thorough manuscript critique.

Many thanks to fellow writers and readers who provided insightful feedback, including Tessa Devan, Phoebe Farber, Salena Fehnel, Liza Frenette, Sandra Galfas, Deivis Garcia, Sharon Gelman, Elaine Insinnia, Emma Larson, Christine Mariani, Kacy Muir, Michael O'Brien, Corinne O'Flynn, Lynne Spease Reeder, Kristi Roberts, Hong Tran, Starr Troup, and Helen Wasiakowski.

I'm also grateful to several people who took the time to offer their professional advice about the literary industry including Debra Galant, Dan Poblocki, Robert Quackenbush, and The Write Group of Montclair, NJ. A big thank you to the Kweli and Las Comadres Literary Conferences for providing indispensable forums for those who believe in fostering diverse voices in literature for all ages.

To Shawn Yaney, thanks for a lovely cover design.

To my parents, Heriberto Ramos and Gloria Pérez, for exposing me to all kinds of stories. To my brother, David, for playing endless mystery games with me when we were kids. To my sister, DeAnna: When I started writing this you were only twelve and you served as an excellent model of a bright and curious tween girl. To my non-blood sister, Jennifer Walz: Thank you for understanding frizzy hair, and always encouraging my creativity.

To all the children and teens I've had the fortune to teach, thank you for letting me learn from your perspective and truth.

And to my wonderful husband, Michael, who read several drafts of this book with the same genuine enthusiasm every time: Thank you for your endless support of my writing habit!

Northampton House Press
and Overdue Books

Established in 2011, Northampton House publishes carefully selected fiction – historical, romance, thrillers, fantasy – and lifestyle and literary nonfiction, memoir, and poetry. Our logo represents the Greek muse Polyhymnia. Overdue Books is the name of our middle grade imprint. See our list at www.northampton-house.com, and Like us on Facebook – "Northampton House Press" – for more great reading!

JY RAMOS

Ramos, Dania,

Who's Ju?

JUN 2 2 2017

CPSIA information can be obtained
at www.ICGtesting.com
Printed in the USA
LVOW11s1053210517
535323LV00003B/525/P

9 781937 997618